Advance Praise for *Compassionate Messenger*:

"Empathic, delightful, humorous, not only reflects Carolyn's personality, but her chosen pathway of life. That she loves her work with spirit is evident, in this enlightening and informative book. An excellent read, full of warmth, compassion, and amusement — all essential ingredients wherever you find yourself on your spiritual journey."
— Jackie Dennison, *Rescue Mediums* (W Network)

"Carolyn Molnar is not only a gifted Spiritualist, but also a captivating writer. In *Compassionate Messenger: True Stories from a Psychic Medium*, Molnar shares her stories about clients, but also her own journey into the spirit world, having done thousands of readings. For many, taking a psychic reading is their first big step into a lifelong spiritual journey. That sense of 'gift' comes through loud and clear in this book."
— Jeff Hurst, editor, *Cambridge Times*

"Carolyn is a popular medium and teacher and I know that her stories will provide insight and understanding of spirit communication. As you read the evidential stories you will know that our loved ones from the other side of life are always with us and communicating in many different ways; we have but to acknowledge them."
— Reverend Sharon Golsby,
president of the Spiritualist Church of Canada

Compassionate Messenger

True Stories from a
Psychic Medium

Carolyn Molnar
with Benjamin Gleisser

DUNDURN PRESS
TORONTO

Editor: Shannon Whibbs
Design: Courtney Horner
Printer: Webcom

Library and Archives Canada Cataloguing in Publication

Molnar, Carolyn
     Compassionate messenger : true stories from a psychic medium / by Carolyn Molnar ; with Benjamin Gleisser.

Also issued in electronic format.
ISBN 978-1-55488-791-0

     1. Spiritualism. I. Gleisser, Benjamin II. Title.

BF1261.2.M64 2010   133.9   C2010-902425-7

1   2   3   4   5   14   13   12   11   10

  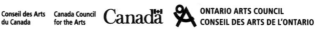

Conseil des Arts du Canada   Canada Council for the Arts   Canada   ONTARIO ARTS COUNCIL CONSEIL DES ARTS DE L'ONTARIO

We acknowledge the support of the **Canada Council for the Arts** and the **Ontario Arts Council** for our publishing program. We also acknowledge the financial support of the **Government of Canada** through the **Canada Book Fund** and **The Association for the Export of Canadian Books**, and the **Government of Ontario** through the **Ontario Book Publishers Tax Credit program**, and the **Ontario Media Development Corporation**.

Care has been taken to trace the ownership of copyright material used in this book. The author and the publisher welcome any information enabling them to rectify any references or credits in subsequent editions.

J. Kirk Howard, President

Printed and bound in Canada.
www.dundurn.com

Dundurn Press	Gazelle Book Services Limited	Dundurn Press
3 Church Street, Suite 500	White Cross Mills	2250 Military Road
Toronto, Ontario, Canada	High Town, Lancaster, England	Tonawanda, NY
M5E 1M2	LA1 4XS	U.S.A. 14150

Mixed Sources
Product group from well-managed forests, and other controlled sources
www.fsc.org Cert no. SW-COC-002358
© 1996 Forest Stewardship Council
FSC

Without Sadie and the thousands of people who have shared their life stories with me, and allowed me to speak with their deceased loved ones, there would be nothing to tell.

Contents

Foreword

I met Carolyn Molnar at a Spiritualist seminar held at a retreat in the North of England. As a physical medium,* I had, by invitation of the organizer, held a séance to enable the delegates — of whom Carolyn was one — to witness communication with the spirit world on a physical level.

Afterwards, I was enjoying a cup of tea in the establishment's tea room when I was approached by a soft-spoken young lady

---

*A physical medium allows a spirit to use his vital living energy, known as ectoplasm, to create tangible physical phenomena outside of the medium's body. Examples of this include the moving of objects, the manifestation of spirit voices, and, the *crème de la crème* of such mediumship, the phenomena of materialisation — the temporary appearance of solid animated phantoms of the dead. A mental medium, such as Carolyn Molnar, uses her five senses to contact the spirit world; all activity is within the mind, and not outside of, the medium.

who introduced herself as Carolyn Molnar from Canada. The retreat was her first experience of physical mediumship, and we chatted together in a manner that was both relaxed and genial.

At that time, my impression of her was in regards to her beautiful accent and of the warm gentleness of spirit that was very evident throughout our conversation. We exchanged email addresses with the promise that we would keep in touch. However, at that time, neither of us could possibly have suspected that out of that meeting would be borne a wonderful camaraderie that would eventually lead to this small contribution to her excellent book.

At this point readers may, understandably, wonder why such a chance meeting should have developed into the warm, respectful, and meaningful relationship that it did. To answer that, I shall make a statement that I know many who possess knowledge of contemporary mediumship will agree with. Conversely, I have no doubt that there will also be many who disagree, because they refuse to face reality and some uncomfortable facts.

However, rightly or wrongly, after forty years of deep involvement in the movement of Spiritualism, I unequivocally believe that Spiritualism today is literally awash with mediumistic mediocrity. It is everywhere, and, as a direct consequence, the movement is the poorer. The reason why standards have so badly deteriorated over the past fifty years can be traced directly to a basic lack of understanding as it relates to the development of mediumship. Sadly, there are many who prefer to bury their heads in the sand. They fail to face reality, and, in spite of their knowledge of the true plight of mediumship and Spiritualism, have convinced themselves that things are not so bad and, that generally, everything in the garden is rosy. My statement, therefore, will find favour with some and not so with others.

Foreword

It brings me no pleasure to record that throughout my own journey, I have repeatedly met with people who simply "wished to be mediums" and most of those, although no doubt well intentioned, sadly failed to understand exactly what the process of development involves. Few ever appreciated that, foremost, mediumship is *always* a matter of sincerity of purpose. Unfortunately, many whom I have encountered merely wished to enhance and elevate their own standing amongst their peers. They suffered from egotism or envied those who had successfully developed their gifts. Indeed, there were a whole raft of reasons for wishing to develop, although seldom were they motivated by "the singular wish to be of service" to mankind on both sides of the great divide. Those who did so for truly altruistic reasons were, in my experience, few and far between.

When I first met Carolyn, I was immediately impressed by her demeanour and by what she had to say. Indeed, within minutes, it became clear that before me was a woman possessing genuine sincerity — someone whom I instinctively knew was a true servant of "the spirit." Throughout that first meeting and later as we exchanged emails, it was always evident that she exemplified what a true channel of two-world communication truly is — or should be. She wanted only to be of service. That impression struck me forcefully and has continued to do so ever since.

In a subject that has been written about exhaustively, this book is a worthy contribution to the literature on mediumship, for it offers the reader a fascinating and unparalleled insight into the life and work of a genuine medium. I was intrigued to read how she came to find Spiritualism, and the gradual awakening and subsequent unfolding of her spiritual gift. Her story, as presented in the following pages, is simply and warmly told, and affords us a fascinating glimpse into her remarkable spiritual journey. We also learn of the people (on both sides of the veil) who entered her own life — who she came to know, and, ultimately, who she was able to help through her own special gift of mediumship.

Often movingly told, the cases that Carolyn has chosen to include in this book play out exactly as she has presented them, free from any form of embellishment. Each experience and each case that she shares with us is remarkable in itself, and had she chosen to simply "gild the proverbial lily," none of the following stories would have dramatically benefited in the telling. Each is unique and will speak loudly and clearly to the reader.

And finally — I firmly believe that she has carefully and painstakingly crafted a book which will appeal not only to Spiritualists, but to a general readership, because each story also offers the gentle reassurance that truly, life, in all its vibrant magnificence, is eternal. Its other function — perhaps not so immediately apparent — is its ability to heal the soul within those readers who know, first-hand, the agony of bereavement, but have little or no conception as to the true nature of life after life.

What Carolyn presents herein should be acknowledged as a faithful record of "a life in service" to the one great truth that life truly is eternal. It will interest the reader on a great many levels, and I am personally honoured to be associated with it.

Stewart Alexander
English physical medium and historian of Spiritualism

○ ○
○ ○

Introduction

○ ○
○ ○

The click of my cassette tape recorder signals that the reading is over. I close my eyes and whisper a quick prayer, thanking my guides for helping me to hear from my client's spirit people. Then I take a few deep breaths to ground myself as I mentally step from the world of spirit back into the world of the physical.

My client, a young woman named Dorothy, has tears in her eyes and a pixie-like smile on her face. Though I don't remember everything I've just said over the last forty-five minutes, I knew Dorothy's mother had come through and had told her daughter she was proud of the great steps Dorothy had taken since she had quit drinking last month. Her father had come through, too, to apologize to his daughter for … well, I'm not sure, but I know they were words Dorothy needed to hear. Her tears and her smile tell me this.

"May I?" Dorothy asks, reaching for a tissue.

"Of course," I say, and nudge the box toward her.

Luckily, Dorothy is my last reading of the day, so I can give her extra time to compose herself. I look away to give Dorothy some privacy, and my eyes settle on the bookcase filled with Spiritualist books, many from the turn of the last century. These precious tomes with worn covers, cracked spines, and titles blurred from use, were bequeathed to me by my mentor, Sadie, in the months before her death. *Take them,* she told me, every time I visited her in her small apartment and, later, at her nursing home. *I am not long for this world. I want them to go to someone who understands their worth.* And so she would gift me with another treasure. These books stand proudly in my reading room, reminding me of the grand dame who taught me everything about connecting with spirit, and gave me the confidence to step into the spirit world and bring back compassionate messages for loved ones in the living. Sadie was a surrogate mother to me, especially after my real mother ...

Dorothy brushes her chocolate-coloured bangs off her forehead and slowly gets to her feet. I thank her for seeing me, and allowing me to serve spirit. As I walk her to the door, I reflect on the thousands of readings I've given as a psychic medium over the last thirty years. All the stories I've heard, all of the lives that have touched me — how enriched I feel!

Most people who come to me are eager to hear from friends and loved ones who have passed on, and are relieved to hear messages that their loved ones are at peace. Yet, others could care less about the spirit world: they want to know winning lottery numbers, or if their spouses are cheating on them, or — can you believe it? — what day they are going to die. Yeesh! Why would anyone want to know that?

My goal is to give my clients information filled with hope and inspiration, but that's not always easy. I remember the woman whose daughter was dying of breast cancer, and pleaded with me to beg her own parents in spirit to let the young woman live long enough to graduate college. She would not let me convince her that I was only a messenger; I can't make bargains with those in the afterlife. And last year, the gay man who visited me — he so desperately wanted to connect with his deceased father and hear from him the words "I love you." He left my office frustrated and hurt, because his father refused to connect with me. And I couldn't in good conscience just tell him something I knew he wanted to hear. Readings like that are tough — how do you try to give hope when there seems to be none?

Before I close my office for the day, I check emails and phone messages. My 10:00 a.m. client wants to cancel his session: car trouble. Ah, but here's an email from a woman who needs to see me immediately — thank you, Universe, for filling the void. Uh oh, wait a minute — the woman is desperate because she wants me to remove a curse that a former roommate has put on her. I wish this woman had included her phone number; I would've called to tell her that she doesn't need a session with me because I don't do curse removal. In fact, I don't believe in curses. You can't be cursed by another person. You *can*, however, curse yourself with negative energy by believing that someone or something else has power over you. As former American first lady Eleanor Roosevelt said, "No one can make you feel inferior without your consent." (I also love her line: "A woman is like a tea bag — you can't tell how strong she is until you put her in hot water.")

Come to think of it, negative energy was what got me started as a medium. Thirty years ago, a woman predicted that my life would come to ruin because of alcoholism, infidelity, and the kind of evil you could only spit at. Would you like to hear that story? Give me a moment to brew a cup of peppermint tea. After work, I like to relax with some fragrant herbal tea while I switch roles from medium to wife and mom. Time to move from the world of spirit to the land of scuffed kitchen floors, an unmade bed, and a sink full of dishes. Housework: now *there's* a curse.

• • •

When I started my spiritual journey, I was seventeen years old, curious and full of wonder about how the world worked. I ironed my long, thick hair because I thought it looked cool. I was tall for my age, and gawky, which came in handy for my role on the defence for my high school basketball team.

That summer marked my first time away from my home in St. Catharines, Ontario, as I travelled with a French immersion class through Ontario as part of a university summer program. When we were in Penetanguishene, a fellow student gushed on and on about a psychic in the area she had visited. The session had been so accurate! The psychic had known so much about her! And this reader had such a great reputation in the community, everyone went to see her! (I kid you not — this girl spoke in exclamation points.)

Then the teacher of the French immersion course said he'd been to see her the week before. He wouldn't tell us what happened, but said the experience of her "psychic powers" was eye-opening. Well, that convinced me. Like any seventeen-year-old, I wanted to know about who I would marry, what kind of career I would have, and would I have a closet full of wonderful clothes to wear?

The psychic — I'll call her Mrs. Ponty — was an elderly lady with a kind face beneath layers of makeup. My first thought was she might have been Mary Kay's biggest client. Perhaps there was a little too much rouge on her cheeks, but her blue eyes sparkled in the light and she showed perfectly lined lips when she smiled.

Introduction

"You would like a reading, dear?" she asked and I thought, *Isn't reading something you do in the library?*

Mrs. Ponty led me to a brightly lit, cinnamon-scented kitchen in the back of her house, and sat me at a small table that was covered with a plain, black cloth. In the middle of the table lay an ordinary deck of playing cards. Mrs. Ponty sat across from me and began shuffling the cards. Her smile was full of grandmotherly trust. As she began talking, I found myself watching her hands, the way her nimble fingers danced through the deck. She flipped those cards like a magician. And I was enchanted by the way her lips pursed in a contemplative frown or curled into a smile when she revealed a certain card. The words seemed to smoothly flow from her, as if someone standing behind her was whispering into her ear what she needed to tell me. Unfortunately, time has dimmed the memory of the messages she gave. Instead, I remember leaving her that afternoon thinking: *How did she do that? When could I come back to see her again?* and *That looked like fun. Can I do it, as well?*

• • •

Fast forward a couple of years....

I was an impressionable young woman of twenty, with my heart tied to a hockey-playing forester I was living with in Nova Scotia — a guy I was pretty sure I was going to marry. On a visit back to St. Catharines, my sister suggested that we see a psychic to find out if my hockey player was "the one," and to learn what kind of career I'd have. (I already had a closet full of wonderful clothes.) We planned a fun outing: we'd both have readings, do some shopping, have lunch, and then go shopping (you can never have too many wonderful clothes).

Under bright blue skies, we drove out into the country. The grassy fields looked like green carpets that stretched for miles.

Spring is truly beautiful in Canada; the air felt fresh and electric. I felt uplifted and alive.

The reader's modest bungalow was on a homey, tree-lined street in the Niagara peninsula. After a couple of tentative knocks on the front door, it opened slowly and a face peeked out. I quickly realized that this woman was nothing like Mrs. Ponty. This psychic — I'll call her Zoe — looked about fifty years old, with wavy brown hair curled down to her shoulders and dark, penetrating eyes. She wore tight beige slacks and a T-shirt. Zoe had a reputation for accuracy — after all, she supposedly worked with the local police. At least, that was the scuttlebutt given to me by my sister.

Zoe smiled and told me to wait upstairs in the living room while my sister had her reading. Then she led my sister away, and I was alone in the airless house. The only sound was the ticking of a clock. But I was excited, because I felt great things were going to be revealed in my reading.

I sat in a wingback chair and stared out through a large picture window facing the street. Sunshine slanted through tree branches. Cars drove by; a mother pushed a stroller along the sidewalk. The scene was quaint, yet standing in Zoe's house, it seemed remote. I felt as if I had fallen into a *Twilight Zone* episode, and something was about to happen....

My sister came upstairs. She looked contemplative. I asked how her reading went and it took her a few moments to respond with a shrug. Then Zoe appeared over her shoulder and waved her hand, gesturing me to follow her downstairs.

I tingled with an uneasy excitement as I followed Zoe. I felt a little dizzy with anticipation, as if I were moving slowly up that first roller-coaster hill, and I'd better grip the handlebar because the downward plunge was coming into view.

And what a view it was. A chintzy, 1960s-inspired rec room with dark wood panelling and a ramshackle bookcase crammed with books, boxes, and little statues against the back wall. There were more candles in the room than in a Catholic church. They flickered in tin wall sconces and on the end tables in the corners. They ran across the top of an old television beside the bookcase. They circled the dark leatherette chairs in the centre of the room, where we sat and faced each other. I almost expected Zoe to start the reading by cackling in a rasping voice, "Cross my palm with silver ..."

She stared into my eyes like she was examining the inner recesses of my brain. After a silence that lasted several minutes, she told me the following facts in a slow, methodical voice: I would not be able to trust my future husband. We would lose lots of money. Financial disappointments and alcoholism would plague us all our lives. He would die young. Each negative pronouncement made me feel more and more helpless and hopeless. And dirty. What a gloomy life awaited me! I felt like I was being cursed.

I felt like screaming.

Then, strange things began to happen.

The wire attached to the television's rabbit ears moved, producing scratching sounds against the wall. Candle flames began jumping in unison, as if the flickering had been choreographed. A book fell off a shelf with a loud thud; a moment later, another thumped to the floor.

Zoe's eyes widened. She gazed into the semi-darkness over her shoulder and muttered, "This has never happened to me." Suddenly, she connected the weird effects to me and gave me a look that felt like the evil eye.

She looked at her watch and said, "That is all."

The room fell silent. I think we were both glad the reading was over.

I walked upstairs with wobbly knees. My stomach churned; my head was swimming; I felt like I was going to be sick. My sister saw how upset I was and rushed me to the door. Zoe said something to us, but we were so focused on getting out of there we never said goodbye. Zoe quickly shut the wooden door behind us.

"Are you all right?" my sister and I asked simultaneously.

I shook my head. She did the same.

"C'mon," she said, and hurried me back to the car. With great authority, she announced she had the perfect cure for our visit with Morticia Addams — shopping therapy!

Later, I was still feeling shaken as we walked through the aisles of the department store. *My fiancé was going to die young?* Everything I saw and touched seemed unreal, like I was watching the world through someone else's eyes. *My future was alcoholism and infidelity?* With my eyes looking inward, I couldn't see the people I was bumping into. *What's the point of going on?* My future, Zoe said, was so bleak. And all of those strange goings-on in the basement.... Was even God trying to tell me I was doomed?

I drifted into the bedding section and held up a package of purple twin sheets. But twins wouldn't fit my bed; I needed a full-sized set. Involuntarily, I opened my mouth and said, "I've got to find a medium."

A medium — what? I wondered. Then: *Who said that?* That low male voice coming from my lips certainly wasn't mine!

My father's face flashed in my mind. I ran to a phone and called him. He was surprised to hear me crying because after my parents divorced, my father and I rarely showed our emotions to each other. But here I was, sobbing as I told him my terrifying experience.

He said calmly, "I have just the person for you. Let me take you to her."

"Just the person" turned out to be Sadie Nickerson, a medium my dad knew about through his wife. A group of ladies my stepmother worked with occasionally got together to meet Sadie for readings. She was always so impressed with the readings that she recommended Sadie to my father, who began making regular trips to see her.

The following Saturday, my father took me to Sadie's apartment in Welland, a small town located atop the Niagara escarpment. Sadie lived on the top floor of a three-storey house that looked like it needed several doses of tender loving care. With trepidation, I walked with my father through a front yard of tall grass and unkempt flower beds. Anxiously, I looked at him. Where was he taking me? *Oh, please*, I prayed, *not another Zoe!*

I rang the doorbell. After I stopped counting my thudding heartbeats, Sadie opened the door. Instantly, my apprehension vanished. Sadie looked like Cinderella's fairy godmother. She had an enchanting smile and permed grey hair that seemed fussed over. She wore a simple loose-fitting blouse and plain blue slacks.

Sadie led us up a series of staircases to her modest one-bedroom attic apartment. She gently told my father to wait in the adjoining sitting room, then invited me into her kitchen and gestured for me to sit at a small, square table covered with a white cloth that was worn, yet clean. Sunshine poured through an open window and sparkled on the linoleum floor. Colourful china figurines lined the shelves. On the counter, ceramic salt and pepper shakers that looked like something from my great-grandmother's house sat beside an earthenware cookie jar. I was tempted to ask if there were any chocolate-chip cookies.

Sadie softly cleared her throat and looked into my eyes. She spoke slowly, soothingly, and asked me about the tears in my eyes. Without thinking, I raised a hand to my cheeks. *Why had I been crying?* I told Sadie about my frightening experience with Zoe: the candles flickering, the wire moving on the wall, and the prediction that my life was doomed to failure.

After I finished, she gave me a gentle smile, then said, "Let's start again."

I burst into grateful tears. Sadie reached out to squeeze my hand and said that what I'd been told wasn't a death sentence set in stone. Someone else's forecast of bad luck didn't have to come true. I could reject it — I had free will to create my own future. Or, if I chose to remain powerless, I could plug into someone else's flawed version of what my destiny should be. I was free to make this choice: I could be powerful, or let someone have power over me.

Sadie — who had never met me — then proceeded to give me evidential bits of information about my life, including the job I was working at, the man I would marry, and a prediction that I'd have two children, a boy and a girl (that one took a decade to come true). There was passion in her voice, and she seemed to care about me. The more I listened to her, the more comfortable I felt.

Then, to make sure I was no longer spooked by the idea of psychic abilities, she said, "Now, you try it."

"What?" I was astounded. "M-me?"

"Yes. Go ahead, tell me something. Something about me. The first thing that pops into your mind."

I closed my eyes and thought a moment. I imagined a cartoon. "I see a red car with snow on it, Sadie."

Her eyebrows jumped. "A new car?" she exclaimed, then chuckled. "I just got one and I have no intention of replacing it."

Fast forward several months: Her "new" car (new for her, but really "used") needed a new part, which made a repair too expensive, so her son drove her to local used car lot. It had started to snow that morning. After much dickering with the salesman, she chose a red Toyota in the corner of the lot — that was dotted with patches of snow! Sadie was so excited, she could hardly wait to call me. "You were right, Carolyn!" she said with delight. "I have a new red car with snow on it — just as you had predicted." I was thrilled, both for Sadie and myself, because my very first reading had come true!

Today, I have to wonder if, on that very first day I had met her, Sadie had sensed my potential as a psychic medium. So I guess I should really be thankful that I received a terrifying reading from Zoe, because the experience brought me to Sadie, who would teach me the fine art of delivering uplifting, compassionate messages.

• • •

Sadie and I worked together for more than twenty years, and in all that time, she never charged me a dime — except for that first reading I had with her. I did try to pay her for her time, for the years we sat at her kitchen table and talked about the importance of working with spirit, and for the weekly telephone calls I made when I was living in Nova Scotia with my then-future husband. But how can you pay someone for wisdom and guidance?

"No," she replied whenever I broached the subject. "You cannot put a price on this." Perhaps her payment was her joy in being able to speak freely about her beliefs, and share her insights with someone who understood her feelings about psychic development and mediumship, Spiritualism and religion, philosophy and science. After all, she lived in a small, conservative town in Canada; not many people shared her views, and that made her lonely.

"Oh, come on," she'd say. "You are a spirit having a human experience. Keep that in mind and you will do your work well."

And: "Remember — always serve. Serve spirit and serve people. That is why you do this work."

And I was an avid learner of all her secrets. At times, I felt like I was the sorceress's apprentice!

As we grew closer with each visit or phone call, I felt something special happening. How could I feel connected so deeply to someone? She told me that not many people understood her, and thought she was aloof. She was impatient with them, but not with me; in our relationship, she was kind and caring.

"What's so special about me?" I asked her one day.

Sadie was silent a moment, and when she finally spoke, her voice was a soft purr. "I had a daughter named Carolyn who died when she was still in the womb," she said. "She would have been my firstborn. I never thought she was lost to me. Whenever I think of her, I imagine a yellow rose."

Her words sent chills down my spine. My wedding flower — and my favourite flowers — are yellow roses.

● ● ●

Sadie's only concern was that I was not exposed enough to others who had the same gift as she did. We all need a variety of teachers, she'd say.

"No, Sadie," I'd chide her back, "you're enough for me."

"But I won't be here forever. You'll find someone to replace me."

"Perish the thought," I said with a shudder. The idea of life without Sadie frightened me. Even though she was forty-four years older than me, she was my mentor, my friend, and my confidante. For twenty years, she was the person I turned to with questions or to seek advice. She gave me the spiritual understanding I needed to move on my spiritual path, and she also became a mother figure, supportive of my work in the true sense that my biological mother was not.

But all things must pass, and when Sadie went into spirit in 2001 at the age of eighty-six, I was crushed. Even though I was — and still am — a Spiritualist who believed in life after life, and knew she had not left me, I felt lost. Looking back, I think what terrified me the most was the thought that I was now alone. I had no one with whom to practise my lessons in psychic development, no one to teach me how to be a better conduit into the spirit world. No one to tell me if I was doing a good job. I was now living the inverse of that famous quote: "When the student is ready, the teacher disappears."

Maybe, I thought, *I should give this stuff up.*

Meanwhile, I had to prepare for Sadie's funeral. Knowing how close she and I were, her son asked me if I would write her eulogy. I agreed, and asked Sadie for help. On the day of the funeral, a thought about her popped into my head at 3:00 a.m. and woke me up. I chided her and told her I needed more sleep and could she come back at 6:00 a.m.? She did. At the appointed time, I sat straight up in bed. Her voice in my ear said, "Come on, get up. We have work to do!"

Later that morning, I was racing down country roads, realizing I would be late for the funeral, when I suddenly heard loud laughter and Sadie's booming voice in my head: "You're going to be late for my funeral." She thought it was hilarious. I did not.

And when it came time to read the eulogy, I spoke without tears the words she had given me (it was hard to cry knowing Sadie was standing by and orchestrating her own funeral). Her family was quite moved, and I greeted them all by name, which surprised them because most of them had never met me before — but I had Sadie nearby to whisper their names to me. Strangers later came up to me and asked how I could know someone like Sadie so well. I thought to myself: *If they only knew!*

As the group of mourners thinned out, I gazed into Sadie's grave and promised her that I would visit her there every year. But two years later, standing at her headstone with tears in my

What is Spiritualism?

*Spiritualism is a government-recognized religion in Canada. According to the Spiritualist Church of Canada (*www. spiritualistchurchofcanada.com*), "Spiritualism is a rational religion based on the proven knowledge that man's spirit survives physical death." Put simply, Spiritualists believe that death is just a transition, and the soul not only continues on, but that loved ones, friends, and even long-lost acquaintances who have passed away are available to communicate with us and support us through life — if we welcome it.*

One of the most important parts of a Spiritualist church service is bringing through proof of spirit. This occurs when a medium connects spirit with several members of the congregation.

Spiritualism is a religion, a philosophy, and a science, whereas "spirituality" can encompass anything from a belief in the divine to a sense that one is connected to the universe.

eyes, I heard her chastising me: *You know better; I'm not here. I'm with you always. Life is for the living, so get on with it!*

(Interestingly, every year since, some type of special engagement has always popped up — sometimes at the last minute — that has kept me from visiting her grave.)

And I have, indeed, gotten on with living.

• • •

"What a long, strange trip it's been," says a line from a song by the aptly named Grateful Dead. That phrase sure describes the experiences I have had along my spiritual journey. You'll read about them in the following stories of my life. They are tales about my students, many who have gone on to become good mediums themselves; stories about what I have learned from my clients (their names have been changed to protect their privacy);

anecdotes about those "Aha!" moments I've experienced in my mediumship and public work; and my times in Lily Dale and England. These stories touch upon love beyond the grave and pain among the living; those who search for answers; and others who lustily embrace the mystery of what makes us human.

Spiritual development, like psychic development, is a lifelong journey, and what we take to the grave is our mind, our personality, our memory, and our soul. So don't believe anyone who says, "You can't take it with you." Because you do. And love never dies. So, remember — you will always be able to tell someone after you're gone "I love you." In fact, go tell that person now. Maybe you have several persons you need to tell. Go ahead, it's important. Be that compassionate messenger. I'll wait.

Thank you, Sadie, and my spirit friends, for believing in me! Our job has just begun.

○ ○
○ ○

Chapter 1

My First Client

○ ○
○ ○

Every time the bus lurched to a stop, my heart lurched in my chest.
And not because I was having a bumpy ride. No, I was scared. I'm
sure I looked as calm as a sleeping baby to the other passengers
on the bus, but inside I was shaking. I could not even remember
the last time I felt this scared. I felt like everything I had worked
toward for the past twenty years might come unravelled. And, for
the first time, I was even asking to be paid for my work! Was it
too late to jump off the bus and run back home?

In the eye of my internal storm — a calming voice in my
head whispered, *You can do this.* I took a deep breath, then blew
it out. I'm sure it sounded like steam escaping from a radiator.
The woman sitting in the seat in front of me touched the back of
her head, then turned around. I looked out the window.

I heard the words again, *You can do this*, and this time I recognized the voice. *Is that you, Sadie?* Then I whispered aloud, "I can do this."

• • •

Over the two decades I had studied and worked with Sadie to learn the art of spirit communication, I grew more confident in my skills. Not only was I giving little readings to Sadie during our chats, but I had begun giving impromptu messages to family members and friends, if an impression or some visual image came to me. And only if they gave me permission. I would never just blurt out something like, "Your father's spirit is here" or "Your mother says those shoes are going to give you bunions." That would be an invasion of privacy — or, worse, make that person feel bad for spending a lot of money on those shoes.

Outside of Sadie, I was a wife, mother, and an office administrator to help pay the bills. When I wasn't developing my psychic and mediumistic skills, I was as straight-up as an elevator shaft. On the job, I was the more organized than a Virgo, as quietly efficient as a Scorpio, and as proper as the Taurus that I am (with Libra rising).

But once past the veneer of the "real world," where I was in a place that I felt comfortable around friends and family, I was not afraid to speak my truth about what I was doing. When people were curious about mediumship, I explained how it worked. Likewise, I told them about my belief in Spiritualism. Though most of my friends and acquaintances have accepted my life choices, others regarded my choice of sideline as somewhat of an amusing diversion, something like taking up falconry or practicing the tuba in the bathtub.

"Oh, you do *that*?" How many times did I hear that? But wouldn't you know it, those who condescendingly gave me those *Oh, that's nice* looks, which made me feel like a toddler who's been patted on the head and dismissed — those nose-wrinklers were the first ones who later took me aside or telephoned me and asked in a hushed voice, as if they were afraid the whole world would hear, "I've got a problem with my _____ (fill in the blank: husband, daughter, boss, cat). What do you think I should do?"

So I told them. It was easy. There was no pressure. I just raised my antenna, mentally said a quick prayer for guidance, and let spirit speak through me. And later, I'd discuss the experience with Sadie.

I must've been doing something right, because friends and acquaintances started coming out of the woodwork to invite me out to lunch, dinner, or high tea, just so they could somehow crowbar into the conversation a question that sounded something like, "Can I ask you, what do you see when ...?" Then I started getting telephone calls that began something like this: "Hi, Carolyn?" [Awkward pause] "I'm a friend of _____ [fill in the name] and I heard that ... well, I was wondering ..." And I'd smile to myself as a picture or feeling began forming in my head. And I had a blast playing the psychic *Dear Abby*.

But then, one day, everything changed.

On July 18, 2001, Sadie passed into spirit.

And my friends and their friends and the friends of their friends kept calling with questions, and asking for advice.

And I had no one to ask for advice.

About a month after Sadie died, I received a phone call from Roberta, a distraught young woman. "I got your name from Bess," she said, flustered. "You've never met me." I was trying to think of who Bess was, when Roberta blurted out, "There's something in my house. I think it's a ghost. Can you come over and take care of it?"

I held the phone to my ear. My mouth was frozen open. *Me?* I thought. *You want* me *to visit and investigate your spirit?*

"How much do you charge?" Roberta asked.

"Thirty dollars," flew out of my mouth.

Pause.

"Okay," Roberta said, and began giving me directions to her house. I scrambled for a pen and paper to jot the info down, then told her I could come over Saturday afternoon, if that was all right. (It had to be: I couldn't ask my boss for a day off so I could "clean" a house. He'd probably think I had become a maid.)

"Saturday's fine," she said and hung up.

A laundry list of emotions tumbled through my body. First, shock: *What have I just agreed to?* Next, giddy elation: *This is wonderful!* Then, pride: *Someone thinks I'm good enough to want to pay me to do this work!* Finally, fear: *What if I can't do this? I'd be too uncomfortable to ask for money.*

I had spoken with Sadie about my dream of someday doing this work full-time, and now I had my first client. But ...

Sadie, the little angel on my right shoulder, was saying, *You can do this.* On my left shoulder, the embodiment of everyone I'd ever met who thought I was crazy (including, at times, myself), laughing at the thought: *Be careful what you pray for; you just might get it.*

• • •

So there I was, sitting at the window of the bus on a sunny Saturday afternoon in July, watching traffic pass at a leisurely clip. Many Avenue Road eateries had put tables on the sidewalk, and people ate and drank and watched me go by in the bus. Oh, how I wanted to change places with any of those folks!

My heart pounded so loudly, I thought it might shake the windows. For maybe the thirty-thousandth time, I closed my eyes and asked my guides for assistance. *Please let me be accurate,* I pleaded. My reputation — what little reputation I had at the moment — was at stake! *Please help me do a good job. Don't let me say anything that will upset Roberta.* Maybe I shouldn't have asked for money. Then I wouldn't be feeling this pressure. *Please help me to talk with the spirit in the house.*

My fear triggered a memory: My daughter was three years old, and I was taking her to the first birthday party she'd ever been invited to. She stood outside her friend's front porch in her new, frilly dress, terrified to enter the house full of strangers and only one familiar face. *What if no one wants to play with me?* she asked, tears rimming her eyes. *What if they don't like me?*

I smiled at her and said, *Of course they'll like you. Just be yourself.*

So I decided to take my own advice.

Roberta's street was the next intersection. I pulled the stop cord and the bus chugged to the curb. I took another deep breath to calm myself, then rose to my feet and pushed open the back bus doors. I never looked back.

Roberta's apartment was located on the ground floor of an old Victorian home that had been broken up into flats. She must have been waiting at the window, because she threw open the door as I walked up the front path. Roberta was a French major at the University of Toronto and dressed the part: comfortable green sweater, peg-leg jeans and curly dark hair that fell in ringlets to her shoulders. Her welcoming smile immediately put me at ease. "Bonjour," I said to her (I had been a French major at Brock University).

She lived in a railcar-styled flat, where all the rooms branched off a central hallway that ended at the back door. Her front room looked as if it had been cribbed together from furniture found at garage sales or at a thrift store. But the area was open and homey. Breezes stirred the yellow curtains in the windows.

As we made pleasant conversation, I looked down the hallway. Suddenly, a formless dark haze flitted across the end of the hall. I stopped hearing Roberta; in my mind I saw a little boy, perhaps seven years old. His auburn hair was cut straight, as if his mother had put a bowl on his head and trimmed around it. He had big, brown eyes, a button nose and chipmunk cheeks. He seemed like a blithe spirit, and I had the sense he wanted to play hide-and-seek with me.

I don't know how long I was staring down the hall, but at some point I heard Roberta ask, "Are you all right?"

I smiled at her and nodded. Then I described what I'd seen. I felt *great!*

"Y'know," Roberta mused, "sometimes I felt like a little kid was watching me. There's a little girl that lives upstairs, and I'd be wondering how she got into my apartment."

"He's not an energy to be worried about," I said, giving her my first impressions. "He's playful, not harmful or hurtful."

As I walked down the hall, I focused on him, and tried to draw him toward me so I could mentally communicate with him. He wouldn't tell me his name, but I gave him mine as I concentrated on the image of him that he had shown me. I had the feeling that he was aware of me, but was hiding — peeking at me from around a corner of the next room.

With my mind, I "spoke" to him gently, as I would talk to any child: *This is Roberta's house. You have to respect that she's living here, too. She's concerned by your running around. When you make noises, you scare her.* In my mind, I saw the little boy come out from his hiding spot, look at me, then melt into the air.

The hallway was deathly still.

After a few moments, I turned to Roberta. "I believe he's gone."

Roberta nodded, then pulled thirty dollars from her pants pocket — a crisp twenty and a ten, each folded in half. I looked at the money in her hand as if she were offering me currency from another planet. I didn't want to take it. How could I? Wasn't I doing someone a service? Roberta could not speak to spirit, so she asked me to. I mean, it wasn't like I was an exterminator fumigating her apartment to get rid of critters. I didn't have any overhead — chemicals to buy, a uniform to wear on the job. Did Bill Murray and Dan Aykroyd take any money in *Ghostbusters*?

Then I remembered something Sadie said — or perhaps I heard her talking to me. *You have to show the universe that you believe what you do has value.* And like it or not, money is the way we show value. Plus, if I didn't charge, would Roberta — or any other potential client who might call me in the future — take me for a serious professional, or regard me as someone who did this work as nothing more than a hobby?

Yes, I was providing a service. And my service was bringing Roberta peace of mind.

So I took the thirty dollars, quickly pocketing the bills, and thanked Roberta for allowing me to help her. On the bus ride home, the money stayed in my pocket; I was afraid to touch it. Later, I put it aside in my room so I could easily get it in case Roberta called back to say the little boy was still around and she wanted her money back. For the next week, I walked around on tenterhooks, and looked nervously at the phone every time it rang, afraid it would be Roberta. I didn't tell any family members or my friends I'd had my first paying gig. I didn't want to feel boastful. And I kept asking myself — have I done the right thing? Did I really help Roberta?

Well, Roberta never called to demand her money back.

But I did begin getting other requests, either to clean a house or from people who wanted me to do a reading for them. And not a lunch invite with the chance to ask a question or two, but a full-on half-hour session where they wanted me to help them discover things about their life. Some even wanted me to help them contact a deceased loved one. For the next year or so, I did about one reading a week, which really helped supplement my meagre earnings as a secretary.

An interesting footnote: three years later, Roberta came to my office for a regular reading. I was happy to see her; I did not tell her she had a special place in my heart as my first client. But I did hesitantly ask her: did you ever feel the spirit presence again? Roberta reported that after my visit, she saw no more movement, or did not hear any bumps or creaks in the apartment. Of course, I felt good to hear that, but by that time, I had grown much more confident in my skills.

One last thought: it's sad today to think there are still people who think that I should be doing my job for free. I get paid to help spirit so I can continue to help spirit. Yet, some disagree. Several years ago, my husband Benjamin interviewed the former host of a paranormal television show which often featured ghost hunters and mediums. After the show was cancelled, the man returned to his roots as a TV news anchor. When Benjamin asked him point blank if he found any of the mediums credible, the newsman rolled his eyes. "They say they're performing a service. But if they really want to help people, they should do it for free." Benjamin countered, "Well, aren't you performing a service by reading people the news? Why don't you do that for free?" Needless to say, that was the end of the interview.

○ ○
○ ○

Chapter 2

Why Do You Want to Know That?

○ ○
○ ○

One of the hardest things I had to learn was how to deliver bad news to a client. Because one of my first readings — as someone else's client — was such a nightmarish experience, I vowed to never put any of my clients through an emotional wringer. But, unfortunately, there are days when sunshine is absent, and not every story ends happily ever after.

I wish I could provide nothing but optimistic news about money matters, health concerns, family secrets, or someone's love life. But I know I need to be honest, and though I always try to offer someone hope, saying everything is a-okay when it isn't won't help someone who is searching for an answer to a worrisome personal problem. Therefore, I answer to the best of my ability any question a client has — except one.

I will not tell someone the day that he or she is going to die.

I learned that lesson after seeing Claudia. I had been a full-time psychic medium for about a year when she visited me. I should have known something was wrong when she knocked on my door. I was in the middle of eating a salad. I scrambled to the mirror to make sure no lettuce pieces were stuck in my teeth, then threw a look at my appointment schedule. Yes, there was Claudia's name — and I could have sworn that when I had looked at that page in my book ten minutes ago, the spot was blank!

A few dainty serviette wipes to my chin, and I opened the door to greet a woman with hazel eyes and strawberry-blonde hair cut boyishly short. She wore jeans and a plain brown shirt. She gave me a hesitant smile, yet her smile seemed cold — not false or unfriendly, but emotionless. My first thought was, *something's missing.*

Then again, I could have still been recovering from my surprise and embarrassment at accidentally overlooking an appointment. "Please come in," I said warmly, and led Claudia into my office. As we sat on opposite sides of my desk, I added, "Thank you very much for coming."

She nodded.

"How are you today?" I asked, getting comfortable in my chair. "Traffic wasn't too bad this afternoon, I hope?"

"Okay."

I waited a moment for Claudia to say more and when I realized nothing more was coming, I nodded and smiled. Then I closed my eyes to centre myself, and prayed for help and guidance from my guides and colleagues in spirit. *Let me be of service to Claudia,* I asked, then opened my eyes and focused on her.

I wondered why Claudia was now facing away from me. Had she turned around in her chair? All I could see was the back of her head. And then in the distance, over her left shoulder, I saw a figure slowly gliding toward us. The back wall of my office was gone, and in its place a limitless horizon, a gauzy grey colour, like the first shade of an approaching sunset.

As the figure came closer, it became an angel. She wore a long black gown that was highlighted in grey, and the silky fabric shimmered in the light as if she were wearing a carpet of stars. She had an hourglass figure and silver wings edged with black. The angel had such a poised, powerful presence, I felt humbled just to be able to look at her.

I was mesmerized by her dark, almond-shaped eyes. They were filled with peace, yet her gaze was searing. She continued to glide closer to Claudia and me. *Why have you come for us?* I mentally asked.

And then I sensed that she was the Death Angel.

A chill rippled down my spine. The angel raised her arms in front of Claudia and Claudia raised hers to meet the angel. They touched hands, and the angel looked away from me to give Claudia her full attention. Claudia rose from her seat, and the angel turned and placed her arm around Claudia's waist. She led Claudia away and the two glided off in the distance, moving smoothly as if they were flying. And then they disappeared.

There was nothing before me except empty grey sky.

Suddenly, I was back in my office, looking at Claudia's face with my mouth hanging open. I felt like I had been staring into space for five minutes, even though my clock showed that about ten seconds had gone by. I shook that vision off, closed my eyes and tried clearing my head. *Show me something else*, I asked my guides. *Give me something that will help Claudia.*

But all I saw was grey sky.

After a few moments, I told Claudia, "I'm sorry, but I'm not able to read for you. I'm sorry you've come all this way, but ..." Lost for words, I shrugged helplessly.

Claudia seemed disappointed — she could not have been more disappointed than I — as we walked to my door. She offered to pay me, but I refused to take her money. I stood at the door and watch her drive off. I felt a deep sadness and a terrible foreboding. *Why did my guides show me that scene? How could that have been useful to my client?* Dazed, I walked back upstairs and looked at my salad. I could not eat. The vision still haunted me and stayed with me for the rest of the evening. I was glad I had no other clients.

That night, I called a good friend of mine, a medium in England. I told her the story, and when I described the angel, I heard a sharp intake of breath.

"Oh, *God,*" she said with a gasp. "That was the Death Angel!"

I had not told her what the angel had telepathically communicated to me.

That night, I tossed and turned in bed, wrestling with the question: *Should I have told Claudia what I had seen? And if I had, would it have done any good?* After all, people have free will to accept, disregard, or change anything I say. I like to tell my clients, "A reading is only as good as the moment I give it." I know of one reader who bluntly told a client she was getting cancer. Horrified at the pronouncement, the client immediately changed her diet, quit smoking, and, the last I heard, has remained cancer-free ten years after the fact. Even though the reader may have saved the client's life, that client has never gone back to that reader because she hated getting such a poorly phrased doom-and-gloom reading.

That client had a strong sense of self, and I admire the way she was able to tell her reader to hit the road. But, unfortunately, there are many clients that think the reader's words are set in stone, unchangeable like a pronouncement from God. I would hate to create in a client's mind a self-fulfilling prophecy: tell someone he will get cancer and he will go home and convince himself that his body is breaking down. Then he gives up trying to take care of himself because — what is the point? He is going to get cancer and die. The world stops being hopeful. Life stops being fun.

I never want any of my clients to feel the same alarm I experienced after my frightening reading with Zoe over twenty years ago, I thought. Looking up into the darkness over my bed, I told my guides I *never* want them to show me death or give me death times.

And they have kept their word.

Yet I still get asked that question. And every time I hear it, I feel sad. *Why do you want to know this?* I wonder. What good would it possibly serve you to know that a certain tomorrow will be your last? I do not care if the person sitting across the desk from me is a terminal cancer patient who may *literally* have days to live, or a healthy, strapping adult who says he is "just curious" about when he is going to "meet his maker." Believe it or not, people say those words to me!

I once met a psychic who said she liked getting that question, and then bragged about how correct she was at predicting death times. I was stunned, and felt like asking her: *how do you find out if you're right?* I hope she does not call the client on that certain day, then grin with morbid satisfaction when the phone keeps ringing.

Even though I can understand why people are curious about their passing — after all, humans are the only animals that are conscious of their own mortality — I do not want to know the moment of anyone's death because I want my clients to always feel like they are in control of their destiny. I do not ever want anyone to stop reaching for a goal they believe is within their grasp. Plus, I do not ever want anyone to get up in the morning and feel dejected. I mean, if you woke up knowing that you only had a short time left on Earth, would you want to do something memorable and help humanity, or would you wallow in despair?

The closest I ever came to breaking my rule was several years ago, when Betty, a caring and gentle mother, came to see me to ask how long Ruth, her teenage daughter, would live. The tenth-grade girl was suffering from lupus, a disease in which a person's immune system attacks the body's own tissues and organs. The disease had weakened her kidneys to the point that she needed dialysis. And Ruth was so depressed, she had stopped eating.

I felt the girl's sickness in my own gut. Betty's tears moved me; I have two children, and could understand her anguish.

"Please," she said, squeezing the tear-stained tissues in her hand. "Tell me … is my little girl going to die soon?"

I did not want to answer her, yet I could not sit silent. I prayed for guidance, asking how I could possibly give this woman hope.

Then I heard myself say, "I see her graduating. You will see her graduate."

The woman stopped crying, and a peaceful look came to her face. She thanked me, but I told her this was spirit speaking through me, not my words. Nevertheless, she was relieved.

Betty kept in contact with me, calling now and then to tell me that Ruth had joined the chess club. A well-known magazine had published one of Ruth's poems, and meditation and yoga classes were easing her daughter's pain. Infections were always a concern. Ruth graduated high school with honours.

That was several years ago. Though I have not heard from Betty, Ruth's name is still on my healing list, and I send her and her mother a prayer now and then. I have a feeling I will never really know the rest of their story, but that's okay. I am just happy I was able to help a mother find peace of mind, and that a teenage girl was able to shake off her depression and prove to the world — and herself — that nothing was more important than achieving a dream. And she worked on her goal as if her life depended on it.

○ ○
○ ○

Chapter 3

Why Can't I Get a Reading?

○ ○
○ ○

When Phyllis telephoned for an appointment, she was curt to
the point of rudeness. Her brusque tone reminded me of some
bosses I had worked for in my "past life." (I was an office manager
at several companies before becoming a full-time psychic
medium.) They treated me like I was uneducated because, in
their eyes, what could I possibly know about the business world?
I did not have an MBA.

But I was patient with Phyllis, as I am with all clients, because
I know that deep down, coldness is often a mask for pain, and
people who are having a hard time processing grief can become
annoyed and frustrated very easily. So I tried to be especially
pleasant with Phyllis, especially when I asked if she would like
directions to my office, and she snapped, "Why, do you think I

don't know how to use a map?" When I did not answer her right away — I was thinking of a tactful reply — she grumbled, "Okay, then, maybe I'll see you Tuesday," and hung up.

I was tempted to erase Phyllis's name from my datebook. Like everyone I know who does this kind of work, there is a small percentage of people who schedule appointments and then do not show up. But I replayed the conversation with Phyllis in my head, and realized her implied threat to not show up was just a ruse to make her feel that she was in control of the situation. Phyllis was hurting and feeling very vulnerable now, and was terrified to admit it. I meditated on those thoughts for a couple minutes and asked my guides what I should do. *Phyllis will see you*, they said, and I wrote her name in my appointment book in blue pen.

• • •

On Tuesday morning, Phyllis appeared for her session twenty minutes early, banging on the door as if her fist were a hammer. *This is going to be trying*, I thought, and took a deep breath to centre myself. I sent her a prayer for healing love, then opened the door.

"Good morning, Phyllis," I said with a smile. "I'm Carolyn."

"Well, obviously," she said and walked in.

There was so much anger around Phyllis that I found it hard to look at her. It was as if her presence took the moisture out of the air and made my eyes sting. *Help me to help her*, I asked my guides, as I led her into my reading room. She sat down and refused to look at me, gazing instead around my office at the bookshelves, paintings, and drawings on the walls, and the huge chunk of selenite a student had given me for Christmas resting atop a shelf. A flicker of a smile crossed her face when she saw the small cloth doll dangling from the ceiling: the fairy godmother from Walt Disney's *Cinderella*, complete with a magic wand.

I tried to make pleasant chatter about the weather and driving conditions (the two favourite conversation topics for people living in Toronto). Phyllis's answers were short and her mood was disinterested. Perhaps it would be best to just get down to business.

Phyllis cradled her purse, a black leather bag that snapped opened with a loud *click*, and pulled out a palm-sized photograph encased in heavy plastic. She tossed the picture on my desk, and stared at me, as if she was daring me to make the next move.

I often ask clients to bring a photograph of the person they would like me to try to contact in the spirit world. I do this because the photo captures the energy of the spirit person, and I can link into that person's vibration to then call in his or her spirit person and wait for a "match." Think of it this way: our spirit is energy, and the spirit world contains millions of energies — just like the stratosphere of our physical world contains millions of radio and television signals. So, focusing all my mental energy on one spirit is like tuning to the right frequency so I can pick up the correct signal and bring that spirit in loudly and clearly.

I ran my fingers over the laminated photograph. "This is your husband," I said. "I feel like he passed from cancer ..."

"Oh, you could say that about anybody!" Phyllis snapped.

I looked hard at the picture and noticed the man's clear, brown eyes, the dimple in his chin and thick, gray hair combed back from his forehead. I tried to pick up some evidence of him, but the muscles in my jaw hurt, and I realized I was clenching my teeth. *Are you doing this?* I asked the picture, but I felt no response. Instead, my arms and legs were aching, as if I were swimming against a powerful tide. *Please let me help Phyllis*, I prayed and waited for information, but my guides were silent. *Where are you, guys?* I asked after a few moments of quiet that seemed to last forever.

I gazed again at the picture. It was like staring at a blank piece of paper.

"I don't get it," I whispered to myself.

Phyllis snorted and I blushed, embarrassed that she might have heard me. "We tried everything," Phyllis muttered. "Naturopathy, reiki, acupuncture, praying, you name it." She reached over the desk, grabbed back the photograph, then dropped it in her purse, which snapped closed. "We went to Sedona and sat for hours in a vortex. A shaman in New Mexico told him to visualize the sun inside his body, burning away the cancer cells and purifying his body. I even bought him a ceramic pin of the sun." She yanked the badge out of the purse and flung it on my desk.

"I don't even know why I still have this silly thing," she said with a snarl. "And I don't know why I bothered coming here."

Phyllis's words stung, and I felt her pain so strongly, I felt like crying. She was angry at me, angry at the unfairness of life because her husband had died, and probably angry at her husband for dying. And that anger was probably keeping her husband's spirit away. Was he feeling guilty for dying? Or did he love her so much that he did not want to appear for her, which would cause her further pain?

Whatever the case, I was stymied.

"I'm sorry," I said after a few moments, "but I can't read for you. I have nothing to give you."

Phyllis stared at me. Her eyes narrowed and bored into me, and then her gaze softened. "Isn't that funny," she said sarcastically. "I just went to another psychic, and she said the same thing. I don't know why I can't get a reading."

I wanted to suggest that she see a bereavement counselor, but as I was trying to find the best words to express myself, Phyllis rose from her chair and walked out of the reading room. She found her way through the reception area and I jumped when I heard the front door slam on her way out.

I sat for a few minutes looking at the now empty chair across from my desk and felt so powerless. And sad that I could not help Phyllis. I had wanted so badly to help ease her pain, but it was impossible to penetrate her energy of anguish. Why would she not let me help her? And why had my guides deserted me?

"I needed you guys, and you let me down!" I yelled. "What gives?"

Just as I was getting angry myself, I heard, *Phyllis did not need your help — she needs something you can not give her.*

Huh?

Sitting behind my desk, thinking about how I could have handled the situation better, I eventually realized that I am a medium, not a grief counsellor. People who are grieving deeply may not be ready to receive information from spirit. Mediumship is not grief therapy, and it should not be used to circumvent the grieving process. People mourning the loss of a loved one need to work through their grief, whether it takes weeks, months, or years. And if grief cannot be faced, then it becomes like a never-ending moment, impossible to get past, and will keep you from connecting with the possibility of love from spirit.

Phyllis taught me a valuable lesson. Today, I have the names and phone numbers of various therapists and healthcare practitioners at my fingertips that I can recommend to clients who need something more than a reading. I can recommend (because I have met and talked with them) bereavement counsellors, psychiatrists, psychologists, certified biofeedback practitioners, massage therapists — you name it.

• • •

Anger or other unresolved emotions stemming from deep, unresolved grief is not the only reason I am sometimes unable to give a client a reading.

Medium Susan Averre told me that she sometimes envisioned brick walls when she began a reading. At first, she wondered if the spirit person was a mason or bricklayer. When that did not feel right, she would then ask her client, "Does a brick wall have any significance for you?" After enough shakes of the head and mystified looks from the client, Susan finally realized that the wall was the message — for some reason, these clients did not want to be read, and had built a wall of security around themselves.

Personally, I don't see walls; instead, when I open my inner eye to look at a client, all I see is a black screen. (This usually happens during psychic readings, where a client wants to know more about a loved one in the living, instead of mediumistic readings, where the client wants to know about someone in the spirit world.) When I see emptiness, I'll then ask the client, "Is this person you're asking about a very private person?" If I get a yes, then I will apologize and say "I'm sorry, I can't give you an answer," because that person is unconsciously blocking me, and trying to penetrate that individual's personal space would be an invasion of privacy. But, I can get other information for clients when it is centred on them, depending on what they want to know.

When it comes to mediumistic sessions, some clients cannot get a reading because they do not know their relatives. This happens a lot. I will bring through a grandmother or uncle who I see in my mind's eye so clearly, I can describe that individual down to the clothes she liked to wear and a mannerism she was known for — as in one case, an elderly lady from Quebec who liked to play the spoons on the front porch of her cabin during the maple syrup season. Grandma came because she wanted to encourage the person I was reading for to develop her musical abilities. But my client just looked at me dismissively and said, "I don't know, I never met my grandmother." Then spirit brought the grandmother's sister, and the client said again, "I never met my great-aunt, I was two years old when she died." Encountering that negativity, spirit pulled back and I really had to struggle to try to deliver a message.

Another example was the time I kept getting a family of spirits who had died in a fire. The smoke was so heavy that I felt it in my lungs. No, my client told me, none of his relatives had died in a house fire. But the family presented themselves so clearly, I saw them standing in a line, and thick columns of smoke rising into the sky. "And why are gold stars so important to them?" I asked, picking up that piece of information. Once again, the fellow shook his head. At end of reading, he seemed very disappointed that he did not hear from his father, Morris, or his uncle, Nathan. My client said he came from a very small family in Montreal and had been eager to hear from Morris and Nathan, the only members of his family to escape from Poland before the Second World War. Most of his other relatives had been killed and then cremated at Auschwitz.

Sometimes, a client wants a certain spirit to come through so badly that he or she does not pay attention when another spirit shows up instead. If grouchy Uncle Ed, who died without telling anyone where he hid the stock certificates, did not like talking to you when he was alive, what makes you think Ed wants to be more friendly and generous toward you now that he is on the other side? (We hope, once he has had a life review, he will change his mind, but you never know.) Other times, the spirit of an old high school buddy or a neighbour wants to touch in with a client, but the individual is so fixated on hearing from Dad, the spirit — and the subsequent message — goes unclaimed.

What is a Life Review?

I believe part of our transition to the afterlife includes a life review, where we watch certain important moments of our life unfold before us as if we are watching a movie. We see the relationships we have formed, decisions we have made, and, most importantly, the results of those decisions — how we have affected others in ways that we could not have known while we were still on the Earth plane. The goal of this experience is to learn from our actions and, hopefully, progress our soul.

The important thing to realize here is that no one judges us during a life review. Instead, we assess ourselves.

• • •

Phyllis was such a difficult experience that, later, I had to find my husband and get a hug from him to ground me.

What makes clients like Phyllis tough for me is they make me realize two things: I am not perfect, and I cannot help everyone. Those are truly humbling thoughts. As a medium, my goal is to serve both spirit and humanity. Yet, in those times where I cannot give a message, I do not feel like I am fulfilling either goal.

And then there are people like Rita, who make me see that it is all worthwhile.

Rita, a thirty-four-year-old single mother from Toronto, had never visited a psychic or a medium before. When I met her for the first time before our session, she told me she didn't know what she was afraid of most — that no one would come through for her, or that someone would.

I took a moment to clear my mind, then told her I was feeling a strong male presence. "I think your father is here," I said.

She seemed confused. "My father is still alive."

How strange, I thought. Not only was I sure that I had her father — the spirit presence, an older fellow with a fringe of silver hair around his bald spot, was telling me so — but he was bringing in someone else for her. "There's another male energy here, a younger man. I'm hearing ... the month of August?"

"August?" Rita pursed her lips and squeezed her eyes, and I knew she was reviewing her mental calendar, wondering who was born or had died in August. "No-o," she said, then sat forward. "Carolyn, maybe this isn't a good idea."

But spirit would not let me go, so I was not ready to give up. *Tell me more*, I prayed, and spirit showed me a cartoon character from my youth: "Augie Doggie?" It made no sense, but I gave what I got. After all, I'm just the messenger.

Rita gasped. "Oh, my," she said quietly. Tears formed in Rita's eyes. "My husband Bill ... his nickname was 'Augie Doggie.'"

With the connection made, Bill began coming in stronger. I described the image I was getting: a tall man who wore a suit in to work every day. Brown eyes. Immaculately trimmed fingernails.

"Did he used to put his hands together like this?" I said, lacing my fingers together and placing them on one knee.

Rita nodded, then said, "Yes. It was a habit he picked up from his father. Oh!" she said, surprised. "Bill's father died about seven years before Bill passed. I wonder if that was the father you were getting."

"Could be," I said. "When I hear father, it might be your father, father-in-law, grandfather, a person who was like a father to you ... or even a priest."

"Please go on," Rita urged.

So I did, and for the next half hour my voice was soft and low, as I seemed to talk in the voice of — as Rita told me later — Bill, who had passed into spirit sixteen months ago. At one point, I had a metallic taste in my mouth — which I've since come to recognize as chemotherapy. (Bill had passed from throat cancer.)

Rita's tears flowed stronger. I closed my eyes and let Bill's words come through me.

"I told you I wouldn't leave you alone," I said gently. "I told you I would never forget you and Mark. You have to have faith. Believe me."

I talked more about Mark, their twelve-year-old son. And I kept my eyes closed the entire time because when I did open them, I felt as if I was seeing Bill's beautiful and loving wife through his eyes.

Bill encouraged Rita to be strong. He said what he needed to say, and then I felt his spirit depart. I silently thanked my guides for allowing him to appear so clearly, and hoped that I was able to give Rita what she needed. She dabbed her eyes, then smiled brightly and thanked me for helping her.

My goal isn't to bring people to tears. My only wish is to bring proof of spirit, and demonstrate that life continues beyond life. Death is not a sad occasion in spirit's viewpoint. The intertwining of grief and memory is what saddens us; that's not only natural — it's something to celebrate. Because our tears prove that we are human.

And after my session with Rita, I realized that one of the greatest lessons we can learn is that grief is of the moment but love is everlasting.

○ ○
○ ○

Chapter 4

"It's About Giving Hope"

○ ○
○ ○

George's eyebrows rose when he first entered my office, and he looked at me as if I were a lump of coal masquerading as a gold nugget. But I was used to this kind of scrutiny from male clients, many of whom gave me "Prove it! I dare you!" looks when they walked in the door. Then they would act like they would rather be anywhere else than sitting on the other side of my desk. But I did not let George's questioning eyes bother me, because I have found that for men, there is nothing worse than admitting that they are hurting. To most men, grief is something you experience for a couple hours, and then get on with your life.

I had been a full-time psychic medium for about three years when George telephoned to book his appointment. He was curt over the phone, but not impolite. I figured that making this call was difficult for him. My clients tend to be about 90 percent female. And there are very few men who work in my field. Why? I've talked to a few (I'm even married to one!), and I think it is because mediumship is an art, not a science, and men need physical, nails-in-the-wall proof to believe; if you can't fold it up and put it in your pocket, it's not real.

George was a tall man with a thick batch of curly hair. As he sat down, he reached into the breast pocket of his navy blue blazer and pulled out a pair of Benjamin Franklin-esque glasses. He smiled, but it was an uncomfortable smile, and he crossed his arms over his chest to give himself a big, comforting hug.

On the outside, his body language was saying "Prove it!" But on the inside, I felt his energy saying, *I want to believe. Comfort me.*

We talked for a few minutes to put him at ease. He was a Toronto Maple Leafs fan and was sure the new goalie would help turn the team around. I joked that the Buds had been turning around so much lately, it was a wonder they weren't dizzy.

Then I closed my eyes to centre myself, and asked my guides to bring clear evidence for George of life after life, and messages of hope to help him. After a few breaths, I felt the presence of a young woman — I sensed she was in her early forties, around George's age. Her long, black hair fell in ringlets that curled around her shoulders, and she had thick eyelashes I would have loved to have on my eyes. She had a warm, loving smile. She showed me a tube of cherry-red lipstick; it was important to her. She then dabbed lipstick on her two front teeth and laughed.

I told George exactly what I was seeing, and did not try to make sense of the image because, again, I'm just the messenger.

"She's telling me you gave her that lipstick as a joke," I continued. "You said her lips were like cherries. At first, she didn't like the colour; she thought it was too bright. But she wore it because she knew you liked it."

George was silent, but there were tears in his eyes.

"And she thanks you for giving her the dark blue dress," I continued. And then I saw her laying down in the dress.

"That was Anna's favourite dress," George said, barely able to choke the words out. "I asked them to bury her in it. I knew she'd want that."

My mouth tasted metallic: the taste of chemotherapy. I mentioned cancer, and George said his wife had died of ovarian cancer, which was first diagnosed in her late thirties. After many gruelling chemo treatments, she went into remission for several years, but the cancer roared back and finally claimed her five months ago.

Anna told me she did not want to talk about her passing. Her suffering was over, and she was at peace now. Instead, she wanted to tell George that she was watching over their two daughters, and was proud of Cynthia, the oldest, for graduating high school *cum laude*. Of course she was at the graduation ceremony; she wouldn't have missed it for the world! And she was happy that her daughter had chosen to wear the butterfly broach Anna had given her for the girl's last birthday.

"She wore it in honour of her mother," George said, blinking back tears.

"And she doesn't want you to declaw Muggles," I said, "even though he likes to sharpen his claws on the sofa. Anna says, 'Muggles is only being a cat.' But she's going to try to work with him so he uses the scratching post you just bought him." I listened a moment, then added, "Try rubbing some catnip on the post."

George laughed deeply. "That cat," he said. After a quiet moment, he said, "Anna was —"

"Is," I said. "She's still with you."

"Yes," he reluctantly agreed.

Our session was over, yet George remained in the chair and looked at the floor. I felt there was something else he wanted to say, so I gave him some time to get ready to say it.

"Y'know, when I came here … well, I came to check you out," he said, then gazed up. His eyes were soft now, kinder. Accepting. "I wanted to see if this stuff was real."

"'This stuff' isn't me, it's spirit," I replied. "I thank spirit every day for working through me so I can serve."

"Well, I'm not going to say I understand it, but …" Again George was silent, and I wondered what he was wrestling with. "I'm a bereavement counsellor and I facilitate for a group that meets in the local Senior's Centre. I wonder if you'd come to do this for them."

His request stunned me. I had never spoken about my work to a group before. What would I say? I am not comfortable standing on a soapbox. I am more at ease in one-on-one sessions with clients. As much as I loved watching John Edward on his television show *Crossing Over*, and secretly desired to do the same thing, I did not think I had the stamina to speak for a long stretch of time and bring proof of spirit to many people at once.

And then I thought — what was the difference between working with one client and being available for many people, but speaking to them one at a time? Here was the chance to help people who were grieving lost loved ones, and I might be able to lessen their pain by showing them that their loved ones were at peace in spirit. And those who had died from debilitating diseases or may have been in pain at their passing could tell the group that they were no longer suffering. Perhaps I could prove that their loved ones were still close by. And as for public speaking — well, I had taken public speaking classes in preparation to help me teach computer courses at community college.

Taking in a deep breath, I told George I would do it, and I was honoured that he asked me.

• • •

I arrived to find the Senior's Centre parking lot (by now I was driving) almost filled. How big was this group?

George met me at the front door. We shook hands and he seemed a lot more relaxed than he had been in our session the previous week. He wore jeans and a polo shirt open at the throat. I was also dressed casually, in slacks and a blazer. At home, as I was getting ready for the evening, I thought it was important to look as "normal" as everyone else in the room. I'm sure some folks were expecting me to appear in a flouncy peasant skirt, a purple sash around my waist, and hoop earrings big enough to toss a basketball through. Nope. That stuff is for the movies. I wanted people to look at me and not be able to readily tell that I was a medium.

We chatted about this and that as we headed into the building. The Leafs had lost again last night, but George was excited about the new defenceman the team had just picked up in a trade. "He's going to turn the team around," George said, and I smiled politely.

He showed me to a small room where I could relax for a few minutes before meeting his group. The room appeared to have once been an office; all that remained were four folding chairs ringing a desk in the centre of the floor. The place looked like it was ready for either a meeting or a poker game. On the desk were a stapler and an unopened plastic water bottle.

George gushed happiness. He was so excited about the turnout! I told him I was glad my line of work had become so accepted — ten years ago, a medium probably would not have attracted more than a handful of people.

"Oh, you've got a lot more than a handful waiting for you," he said. "I think we've got about fifty people tonight."

I almost swallowed my tongue. Fifty people! *Fifty people are expecting messages?*

"And they're really looking forward to this," he added proudly. "I told them all what a great session I had with you."

Fifty people!

George told me he'd be back for me in about ten minutes, gave me an encouraging pat on the shoulder, then went to tell his group that I had arrived.

Dazed, I sat in one of the plastic chairs and unscrewed the cap off the water bottle that had been left for me. At least, I hope it had been left for me. The small room grew tinier by the minute. *Fifty people!* And each one of them was hoping to hear from a loved one who had died. Would I have enough time and energy to get to them all? I would hate to disappoint anyone — but I knew I inevitably would. Even John Edward talked to only three or four people in his audience of a hundred on his half-hour show. How could I possibly reach fifty?

Nervous and scared, I begged my guides for help. *C'mon, guys, be strong with me.* I looked at my watch: seven minutes to go. I closed and prayed my head off. *Please help me reach these people. Please help me ease their pain and grief. Show them that there is life after life.*

After what felt like several minutes, I opened my eyes and took a deep breath. *Let's do it*, I thought, then turned to see George standing in the doorway, smiling at me. I flashed on the last time he had seen me, in my office. Well, who was the nervous one now?

"Let's do it," I said.

We walked into a room about half the size of a high school auditorium. The first thing I saw was a gallery of eager faces.

Young and old, male and female, impeccably coiffed tresses and hair that needed trimming, and each pair of eyes looking at me hid a story of loss. Yet I did not feel like crying. I felt hope — these people sitting silently on undoubtedly uncomfortable folding chairs were looking for hope. And I knew in my heart that I was going to do my best to give that to them.

The back of the room was cordoned off by accordion doors. I was introduced and stood at the dais with my index cards, which I had used to prepare for my talk on mediumship by writing down a list of salient points. My hands shook a little, but I was calm. I smiled at the expectant faces and noticed the boxes of facial tissues spread throughout the room. *Okay, guys*, I thought, *I trust you. All will be well.*

Suddenly, square-dance music filled the air. Several people sucked in their breath with annoyance. I felt for a moment like I was back in Cape Breton. I did a little do-si-do on the platform to lighten the mood. With a look of horror on his face, George bolted from his seat and ran to the accordion doors to see what was happening. A square dance group had booked the other half of the auditorium!

"Oh my God," he said, "I'm so sorry. If I'd known, I would've scheduled the group for another day. I'll tell them to stop —"

A heavy metal concert would have bothered me; happy-go-lucky fiddle music I could handle. "Don't worry about it," I said. "Once I get started, I won't even hear it."

And that's exactly what happened. I began explaining my work, and in my ears, all distractions vanished. After my brief introductory talk, I asked for questions. No one raised a hand. Very well. I thought a quick prayer to the Infinite Intelligence, and asked my guides who I should speak with.

As I scanned the room, I noticed someone who appeared to be glowing. It was a soft glow, as if a small flashlight had been aimed at that person, and then the individual became phosphorescent and the glow surrounded that person's head like an aura. *Okay*, I thought, *I need to talk to you.* Then I asked that person, "May I come to you?" As a medium I do this to not only ask permission of the person, but to establish a link between myself and my guides, and the individual and his or her guides. (I work a little differently now, and I'll explain that method in a later chapter.)

"Yes," the person answered, and the louder the answer (within reason), the better the connection. I would use the sound energy the person gave me to help establish a connection with the spirit associated with that person. Think of it this way: your voice is like a key that will open a door to a house, and inside that house live your spirit people — friends and loved ones. But if you do not give me that key, or if your key is brittle or you do not believe your key will work — well, it won't.

But what's interesting, at least from my end, is when I'm surprised to discover that the key will fit a room that I never knew existed. Which is what happened that night, time after time.

What was good: when I started bringing forth spirit people and giving messages, I was able to focus on the individual in the audience and when I talked to her, it was as if she and I were alone in the room. My antenna was working well. And when we finished, I was easily able to find the next individual by glomming onto the next glow.

What was not good was that throughout the evening, I never seemed to be able to get the spirit person that the audience member wanted to hear from. Instead, I would get someone's friend or acquaintance. Like the woman who wanted to hear from her daughter; instead, I brought in the daughter's roommate in the hospital. The woman was clearly able to recognize the daughter's roommate from the evidence I gave, but as I was speaking to the woman, I felt as if she wanted to say to me, *Why do I want to hear from this person?*

Another example: I did not connect with the boy, but the audience member heard from a next-door neighbour who had watched the boy playing in his yard. And on and on it went like that; I was one off all night, and through it all, only one person cried.

The event was a disaster.

I felt like a failure. I had let everyone down. They had come here to hear from lost wives, husbands, and children, but I'd brought army buddies, old schoolmates, and somebody's milkman. My face burned brighter than any glow I had seen from the audience. When George rose from his seat to announce that it was time to close the evening, I felt like fleeing.

Polite applause made me feel even worse.

Yet I thought I would seem cowardly to just disappear. So I took my time with putting my note cards back in my purse and drinking from my water bottle. People began coming toward the dais and I stayed to greet them. I wondered if I should apologize to them.

A man and his wife shook my hand and thanked me for coming. *Really?* I thought. They seemed happy and as I listened to them, I suddenly went into the zone.

"You have a daughter in spirit," I said. "She passed from leukemia. In the hospital, she was shuffled around in different rooms." The couple nodded, enthralled. "She wants to thank you for taking such good care of her. She knows it must have been difficult." A tear rolled down the mother's cheek. "She says she came to you last night."

She swallowed hard. "Yes, I dreamed about her. And this morning, I prayed that I would get a sign that it was really her." The woman looked at her husband, who put an arm around her, and then she took my hands in hers. "Thank you."

The next woman in line, an older lady in a red hat, asked how long I had been practicing mediumship. I was about to answer when I heard a man playing a trombone — very badly. I told the woman this. She grew wide-eyed, and put a hand to her mouth.

"He liked to play along to Lawrence Welk," I said. "He's thanking you for putting up with it. And sometimes, he put the instrument down and danced with you. He says you were the better dancer."

She smiled and with the back of a hand, she wiped her eyes. "I was," she said with a grin.

And so it went for the dozen or so people who had sought me out afterward. I gave them messages from loved ones — messages that should have been given during the event, where I could have really shown people plenty of "Aha!" moments and proved the existence of spirit. Instead, I was giving people twenty-second mini-sessions.

The last person waited patiently until all the others had gone. She leaned toward me and said in a conspiratorial voice, "I see auras. And while you were up there giving messages, the whole back of you was glowing yellow and white. The light was completely around you, and it was enormous. And the light changed shape when you were finishing or starting another message. Thank you. You made me feel like all this was real."

I suppose that should have taken the sting out of what I had been feeling that night, but it didn't. I was angry. Driving home, I yelled at my guides: "How could you have made such a fool out of me in front of all those people? Not one person got what they were looking for." I was so steamed that I pulled into a Tim Hortons and ate two chocolate donuts.

Driving out of the Timmy's lot, I heard a calm voice in my head. *This was not about you. This was not about grief. This was about hope. Tonight, you gave these people hope.*

Did I? I thought about spirit's message to me. If these grieving people had heard from who they had hoped to be contacted by, there would have been a lot of crying and they might not have received the overall message that, yes, there is life after life. They had all received confirmation that life continued past the transformation we call death, and their loved ones in spirit were part of a community filled with others who loved them. And that made me realize the wisdom of spirit. The spirit does what they think is important, not what I think is important. They have higher ideas and a better idea of how to accomplish them.

And reflecting back on that night, it also gave me hope for myself. I realized I was a pretty decent speaker before large groups of people. For sure, walking up to the platform was a throat-grabbing moment, but once past those three seconds of sheer terror, and knowing my guides were with me, the experience was fun. I came, I trusted, I spoke. And I wanted to do it again. I began volunteering to work as a medium at Spiritualist churches, where the service includes proof of spirit. Later, I began organizing public message events, and I worked public message services at Lily Dale, which I continue to do to this day — and where I hope to see you eventually. (But more about Lily Dale later.)

Yet, old hand that I am now at speaking before people, I still get butterflies whenever I hear my name being announced, and I walk to the front of the church or hall. Because I know they're in charge, not me. And I continue to trust.

Chapter 5

Medium or Mind Reader?

I recently taught a beginner's mediumship development seminar at a bookstore and spiritual centre outside Toronto. As I was tidying up after class, I noticed out of the corner of my eye a young woman waiting until everyone else had left the room. She had a curious yet thoughtful look on her face. Often, a student who's new to psychic development will linger until we are alone, then tentatively approach and ask me in a hushed voice, "Is this stuff really for real?" or "Am I going to start seeing dead people?"

"Carmen," her nametag read. Carmen was in her mid-twenties, and her feathered hair was the colour of night sky. Her beautiful dark eyes gave her an inquisitive look. She had not talked much in class, instead spending her time taking studious notes during the lecture portion of the three-hour seminar. And she seemed to enjoy working with her fellow students when I paired them up for group exercises.

I smiled at Carmen as I reached for a cup of herbal tea — my voice was rough — that the bookstore owners provided for workshop participants. Carmen munched on a chocolate-covered graham-cracker cookie, and thanked me for an interesting presentation. And then my student said something that floored me.

"When you do mediumship," she asked, "how do you know you're *really* speaking to someone in spirit, and not just reading someone's mind, or picking up something in their aura?"

I stopped what I was doing to consider her idea, which was actually a question I sometimes ponder myself. Even though I have been a medium for more than thirty years, and I believe in the wisdom of spirit — I occasionally wonder: where does the information I give come from?

Carmen and I walked across the street to a coffee shop to discuss this subject. Over café lattes (decaf for me, please!) and bran muffins, we came up with three possible answers to Carmen's question:

1. I get information by accessing a person's Akashic Record, which is basically a storehouse of information about that person's soul;

2. I pick up material from my client's etheric aura, that area around the body which contains information about a person's energy, and stores the person's experiences, emotions, earthly and karmic relationships, possibilities, etc.; and/or

3. I communicate with my client's guides, angels, deceased loved ones, friends, pets, and whoever else happens to stop by and say hello, and these beings give me the information.

"This is interesting," Carmen said, opening her bright green spiral notebook. "I want to write this down."

Going over my responses again so they could be recorded for posterity, I chose door number three, and here's why. First, I'm not an Akashic Record reader — I'm not trained in that art and, besides, to open the book of someone's life and read about that person's soul progression, I would need that individual's permission. It would be like going to a library without a library card — the guard at the front desk would stop me from taking any book out and tell me to get a card.

As to reading an aura: yes, it does contain lots of useful information that I can psychically pick up and give a client. After all, a psychic reading consists of just that — having your aura read. However, what I can pick up from an aura is limited. Think of your aura as a layer of light that surrounds you; as you move through life, all the bits and bobs that enter your light — your experiences and emotions — are what I intuitively see around you.

Your aura also contains possibilities — events that might happen — but because you have free will, those events may never occur. For example, a person who lets himself get "eaten" by stress may develop cancer. However, if he learns to calm himself through meditation, chooses a nutritious diet, and embraces exercise, he may avoid developing that debilitating disease.

But what about when I give a client information that she — and, obviously, me — cannot possibly know before we have met? Where does that knowledge come from? The only answer I can think of is the knowledge was given to me through the client's angels, guides, and loved ones who have passed into spirit. These presences want her to know this information because it is important. So they speak to me, and I deliver their messages for them.

(I rather enjoy the idea espoused by the ancient Greeks, who believed that pieces of news and gossip had energies of their own and could fly through the air. Hence the phrase: "A little birdie told me.")

I remembered a reading I had once given to — let's call her Doris — where I received information from Doris's grandmother in spirit. She told me to tell Doris that she should be aware of a genetic predisposition to a blood disease in Doris's husband's family. Even though this condition had been dormant for several generations, it might affect Doris's eight-year-old daughter. Doris looked at me like I was speaking Swahili, but four weeks later, she emailed to tell me that doctors had just diagnosed a possible blood disorder in her young child. Thankfully, the doctors had caught it in time.

"How did you know this?" Doris wrote, before she signed off.

My email reply to her: "I didn't. Your grandmother is watching over you. Thank her."

Carmen considered the story while twirling a lock of hair in her fingers. "But if the blood disease was part of the family, might it still have shown up in her aura?"

"The disease was part of Doris's husband's family, not Doris's."

"But when she married her husband, didn't his aura become part of hers?"

"No. We are individuals and carry our own energy."

I mentioned a reading I had given at a recent public message event. I had brought in an Italian aunt of a woman in the audience, and I presented evidence of spirit by describing the spirit lady down to the clacking rosary beads she always carried in her pocket and the mole on her chin. The woman had loved her jolly Aunt Esme, and was happy to hear that Esme was watching over her. "Esme's laughing," I told her. "She says you burnt the cannolis. She's saying, 'Shame, shame, I woulda never burned the cannolis!'"

What are the Akashic Records?

Picture a huge library, with crowded bookshelves that stretch farther than the eye can see. Each book in this great library contains the record of one soul's thoughts, words, and deeds throughout that person's life. We write the history of our lives, the philosophers say, and in the case of the Akashic records, this is true.

The word Akashic *is Sanskrit for "air" or "ether," which implies that this cosmic record of humanity exists in another dimension. When we transition into the afterlife, we are permitted to see our "book of life" as part of our life review. Some believe psychics are able to access the Akashic Records to help give people insights into their life. Others believe we can access our "book" in our sleep through our subconscious, because the Akashic Records exist as the collective unconscious.*

The entire audience was laughing, and no one harder than the woman I was speaking to. "That's right!" she said. "They came out of the oven looking like little pipes!"

Later, at that same event, I gave another woman the message that Arlene wanted to say hello. The woman looked at me blankly. Arlene had passed away in September 2006, I added, and she said that she was with a man named Frank. The woman in the audience shrugged.

Two days after the event, I received an email from her: while going through her jewellery box yesterday, she pulled out a pearl necklace her mother had given her years ago. It was given to her by a man named Frank, the first man she dated after her parents divorced — which came as a result of an affair her father had with a woman named Arlene!

Other times, spirit information seems to come out of nowhere, like when I open my office door to greet a client and immediately feel a happiness wash over me. "Oh," I'll say with a smile, "I smell jasmine — your mother is here," and my client asks, "How did you know my mother's favourite perfume was jasmine?" And so our session begins as more personal evidence comes through before we even sit down to formally talk.

I gave these examples to Carmen, which my inquisitive student accepted with a contemplative nod. Then she asked, "So you can just walk around and pick stuff up from people?" She looked around the coffee shop, and gestured with her chin to an older fellow sitting at a corner table, reading a newspaper. "What spirit person is with him?"

"I won't enter his personal space without his permission." Then I laughed, stood up and collected my things. "Besides, the meter's not running. I'm off duty now." I said goodbye to Carmen and wished her well. What I did not tell her was her mother in spirit was glad she was beginning to explore her spirituality.

Chapter 6

Going Gently Into That Good Night

Shoshanna stayed after class, waiting until all my other students were on their way to their cars, before she asked me if I could help her dying co-worker and friend, Nicki, who had entered hospice. Nicki and Shoshanna worked together at a Canadian social service agency, where Shoshanna was the office manager. At that time, I had been teaching a psychic development class for several months; half of my ten female students were clients who had asked me to help them develop their psychic skills, and the rest were people who had found me through friends or by word of mouth. Shoshanna was in the latter bunch.

I was a medium, I reminded Shoshanna. My experience is with those who have passed away, not with those who were preparing to pass.

Shoshanna quickly apologized for giving me the wrong impression. "I'm not looking for you to work with Nicki," she said. "I'm trying to create a community of women to support her through this." Nicki was sixty years old, and her husband had died of lung cancer three years earlier. She had an older sister living in Toronto, and two married daughters living in Edmonton and Vancouver. "We're working together to help take the load off her family," Shoshanna added.

I told her I would be glad to help. "What would you like me to do?"

Shoshanna grasped my hand in gratitude. "Just be there."

She explained that Nicki was a very spiritual woman and had turned to Buddhism throughout her illness. I confessed I did not know much about Buddhism, and Shoshanna admitted that neither did she. "But I know Nicki, and that's enough for me."

Later that evening, Shoshanna telephoned. She had just spoken with Nicki, who was very eager to see me. When could I come by?

• • •

To prepare for my visit, I Googled "Buddhism" and found as many different explanations of the religion as the number of Buddhist websites I found. I was especially interested to learn about how Buddhists view the afterlife. One site talked about the progression of the soul, while another stated that Buddhism focuses more on the present, because what one strives to accomplish in life is much more important than what could ever possibly occur after death.

I learned that two of Buddhism's main tenets deal with suffering and the impermanence of life. Basically, life contains suffering because human nature, and the world we live in, is not perfect. We suffer physically through pain, illness, injury, old age, and, ultimately, death; and we suffer emotionally through sadness, fear, frustration, and regret. Yet life also offers more than suffering — we can undergo positive experiences like joy, peace, and laughter. However, difficulties arise when we attach those positive feelings to objects, because our imperfect world is subject to impermanence, which means we are never able to permanently keep those wonderful objects that we have strived so hard to earn. For example: the car you worked so hard for to buy? Gone in a moment, stolen by some thug. Or the top management promotion you put so much effort into winning? *Poof!* You get laid off a month later, due to a recession.

And one day, we will pass away, too. Because just as that car or that great job is an attachment, so too is our body an object of attachment. To think otherwise is a delusion, because what we call "self" is just cosmic dust that our energy has shaped into a body. And that body is not ours to own — it is merely a part of the universe.

Whew! Thankfully, I encountered the teachings of Vietnamese Buddhist monk Thich Nhat Hanh, who put it all into perspective by stating: "Nothing remains the same for two consecutive moments." In other words, when you understand that life is all about change, you realize that anything is possible — and you can change (hopefully, for the better). Unfortunately, some people resist change out of uncertainty and fear, which then creates suffering. "When a flower dies," writes Hanh, "you don't suffer much, because you understand that flowers are impermanent. But you cannot accept the impermanence of your beloved one, so you suffer deeply when she passes away."

As I got dressed the next morning in preparation to see Nicki, I wondered if I should write all of these Buddhist ideas on note cards so I could speak intelligently on the subject. After all, I did not want to appear as if I were uninformed. But I heard the voice of reason in my head, *Don't think about yourself, concentrate on helping your friend.* So I made my morning fruit smoothie and left for the hospital.

• • •

I walked into Nicki's private room and met Elaine, another member of Nicki's support community. Elaine and Nicki had gone to university together and stayed in touch over the years. Elaine had vibrant red hair and the handshake of a weight lifter. She wore a white A-line dress, and the turquoise-coloured scarf knotted at her throat set off her grey eyes.

Nicki's purple scarf covered the top of her head. She lay in bed with her head and shoulders slightly raised, and her small body was like a stick figure under the bright white bedcovers. Her skin was an ashen colour, and her thin lips were stretched tight, as if her mouth were in a constant state of dryness. She did not resemble the joking pixie that Shoshanna had described. Yet there was a sparkle in her eyes, as if the playful spirit within her was crying out, *I haven't given up yet!*

Beside her bed, beeping machines monitored her heartbeat, breathing, and other functions. On a dresser, beneath a window that overlooked the hospital entrance, was a long-necked vase of marigolds and a gold-framed picture of Nicki, dressed in a forest-green pantsuit and surrounded by her children and grandchildren. The pixie in her was strong in that photograph, and her toothy smile made it seem like she had just heard the funniest joke in the world.

"Hello, Carolyn," she said, whispering with an old woman's voice.

"Hi, Nicki." I tried to smile, but I'm sure it looked forced. I was so hesitant about saying something that might come off as rude or insensitive, I said nothing.

"You're a psychic," Nicki said. "That sounds fascinating."

"Yes, it is."

"Come closer," she said, and I was embarrassed to realize I was still standing by the door, as if getting ready to beat a hasty retreat. "You're also a Spiritualist. How is that different than being a psychic?"

I pulled a plastic chair from a corner of the room and placed it beside Nicki's bed. Spiritualism, I told her, is the belief that we never really die, because the soul continues to live after the body ceases to function. Our body is matter, our spirit is energy. And, further, when we are freed from the weight holding us to the physical world, we can use our energy to help those in the physical realm. Nicki listened, enraptured, and I was amazed at how comfortable she was talking about death and dying.

"And you go to a Spiritualist church?" she asked. "Tell me about the ceremony that you do."

A Spiritualist service has three parts: a lecture (or, as they say in England, "the philosophy"), usually on one of the Seven Principles of Spiritualism; mediumship (in England, "the demonstration"), where a clairvoyant will bring evidential messages from spirit to some congregation members; and spiritual healing. Nicki seemed especially interested in the last aspect, so I explained that spiritual healing was energy work, similar to reiki. The goal of the healing was not to create spontaneous healings of a physical nature, but to fill one's soul with a sense of peace. The healer becomes a conduit of healing energies that come from a higher source, and moves his or her hands around the person's body in a kind of touchless massage. The healer and the individual sitting for the healing often pray for divine help and guidance during the experience.

"Would you like to try it?" I asked.

Nicki smiled hopefully. Elaine wanted to help, so I told her to stand on the other side of the bed and focus positive energy on Nicki. I stood up, closed my eyes, and concentrated, fixing in my mind the image of Nicki lying on her bed and filled with serenity. Mentally, I said a prayer to Archangel Raphael, the healing angel who helps stimulate life energies and higher mental energies, and asked for help and guidance.

I imagined the palms of my hands filled with peaceful energy. I placed my hands about six inches above Nicki's scalp, then slowly moved my hands down over her forehead, sending warmth and gentle chi — the energy of the universe that is present in all living things — into the third eye region of her brow. I moved my hands down over the blankets that covered the top of her body, then slowly down her torso, sending cleansing energy into her chest, her hips, her thighs —

Sudden my hands flew up off her, as if something had swatted my arms away. I looked in astonishment at the bedcovers over the region of her left thigh. It had sharply rejected my hands, the same way two north ends of a magnet repel each other. Both Nicki and Elaine were just as amazed.

"That's where the cancer is centred," Elaine said. "On her left leg." (Later, she told me the tumour was the size of a football.)

Dazed, I sat back down. I had never experienced anything like that before. I needed a moment to collect myself.

"What else can you tell?" Nicki asked, "Can you tell me what day I'm going to die?"

I swallowed hard and forced myself to look Nicki in the eye. "I'm sorry," I said. "I've asked my guides to never to reveal death time to me. I want my work to support life, and when you know that information, it takes away from the living."

Nicki nodded pensively. "I understand that, but I'd still like to know my date. So I can prepare myself better."

But if you know the exact date, I felt like arguing, *wouldn't that make the event permanent? And doesn't Buddhism teach the impermanence of life, so you are always free to change and shape your own destiny?*

But I said nothing.

Nicki asked, "What will happen to me after I die?"

Flashing lights outside the window distracted me for a moment. An ambulance was pulling up to the emergency room doors. I had a feeling the victim had suffered a stroke; I did not want to know any more.

I turned back to Nicki. "I don't know for certain," I said. "It's still not super clear to me." I put my hand on her blanket, where I thought her hand would be. "I believe we go into the light, but after that I don't know."

"You don't know. But what do you think?"

"Remember … everything I'm giving you is theory. I won't know for sure until I go home, which is heaven for me. But I've heard that we stay around the Earth plane for three days to check out how our funeral goes, and see how people are affected by our passing. But I do know this," I said, leaning toward her. "We don't pass into spirit alone. Our relatives come to greet us so we're not scared. They wait for us and help us prepare for the transition."

Nicki quietly digested this, then asked, "Do you see anyone with me now?"

I closed my eyes and concentrated on seeing with my mind's eye. The room seemed filled with indistinct shapes. "Yes, I do sense a lot of people around you."

"How do you know this?"

"The same way you know that I'm with you now. Let me try to describe the lady standing at the foot of your bed. She's rather strong-willed, like she's a guardian. But she's also waiting to give you support." I tried to get her name, but she would not give it. "I'm sensing an aunt. Very headstrong." I tried pulling for some physical description, but the spirit was relentless. She would not even look at me; nothing was more important than Nicki's welfare. "But she always had a soft spot for you."

Nicki lay still. Then her thin lips twitched and slowly curled into a smile. "Yes," she said. "Yes."

She closed her eyes and breathed gently. "That was most interesting," Nicki said. "Thank you for coming, Carolyn. I'm getting tired now." Elaine and I turned to go, but Nicki said, "Elly, wait a minute. I need to talk to you about something."

We said goodbye and I left, wondering if my visit had done anything to help her. I had gone not knowing what to expect, and I was grateful not to find a bitter woman filled with tears and grief and defeatism. She seemed so accepting of her death as the next step in her soul's progression. Yet I also felt sad and helpless, because there really was nothing I could do for her except talk and listen. The spiritual healing had not seemed to bring her any peace. Maybe all she needed was someone to talk with. Still, I had hoped to do so much more.

And, I had no idea if I would see her again....

• • •

Several mornings later, Shoshanna telephoned to say that Nicki had really enjoyed my visit, and had asked if could come again and speak with her. I told Shoshanna I was free this afternoon, and I would visit as soon as I finished pulling all the blankety-blank tent caterpillars off the leaves of my rose bushes. I hated those critters for finding my rose bushes so tasty. I had nursed those plants through frosts and draughts, and I was determined not to let a stampede of upstart worms kill my flowers!

This time, Nicki and I did not talk about death, we talked about life. We compared aspects of Buddhist and Spiritualist philosophies, and how each stresses impermanence — change — as something good. We agreed that challenges that test our mettle offer us the opportunity for spiritual growth. As concentration camp survivor Viktor Frankl said, "When we are no longer able to change a situation, we are challenged to change ourselves." In other words, when we are challenged by an experience that we cannot change, then we are challenged to change ourselves to fit that experience. And every learning experience presents us with the chance to progress our soul.

"Change is something more than what you find in your pocket," Nicki said with the hint of a smile and playfulness in her eyes.

I enjoyed spending time with Nicki. She made me feel valued, as if what I said was important to her. And even though she was bedridden and under pain management, she never lost herself to the trappings of cancer.

When we said our goodbyes that afternoon, I took her hand and tried not to cry. I had a strong feeling that I was saying my final goodbye to her in the flesh. I did not want to get emotional, because I knew Nicki did not want pity or sympathy. So I left with an ache in my chest, wishing there was something more I could have done for her.

But even mediums who think they're always right are often wrong, and a few days later I was happily surprised to hear that Nicki had once more asked Shoshanna, "Can Carolyn come in again? I'd like to speak with her." I cancelled some appointments to make time to go.

● ● ●

I was brewing a pot of chai tea when I received the call that Nicki had died. Shoshanna spoke very slowly, and there were tears in her voice. I felt as if the world had suddenly stopped spinning. I was standing in the kitchen with an empty mug in my hand and a lump of sadness in my throat. Shoshanna and I continued talking, but I cannot remember what we said. All I know is that at some point the conversation ended and I hung up the phone.

Time passed.

The tea kettle whistled and I looked again at my empty cup.

Why am I so surprised? I wondered. *All things must pass.* And then I thought of this line from Woody Allen: "I'm not afraid of death — I just don't want to be there when it happens." Being a medium and a Spiritualist, I do not fear the transition we call death — but that moment when we undergo the transition from physical to infinite will always mystify me.

I said a prayer for Nicki, and hoped that in the short time that I had known her, she had thought of me as a friend. *Go with peace, my friend. Namaste.*

• • •

The funeral home was packed. I met the rest of Nicki's community of women and we sat in two rows in the middle of the room. A Buddhist priest led the ceremony, and I was surprised that he was not a bald, wizened-looking Asian man in a saffron-coloured robe. Bob was bearded, had thick, dark hair, and wore a suit and tie. There was no coffin or box of ashes on display, either. Just Nicki's picture and Bob the priest talking solemnly about life and the changes we all undergo. Though the mood was upbeat, many people were weeping.

I was sitting in an aisle seat. All of a sudden, I saw a blur of air *whoosh!* by. The haze flew up and down the aisle, then over my head. As it hovered over me, I heard a voice in my ear: "I'm here." It was Nicki's voice, but not the hoarse whisper I was used

**The Seven Principles of Spiritualism,
as Set by the Spiritualist Church of Canada**
1. *The fatherhood of God.*
2. *The brotherhood of man.*
3. *The communion of spirits and the ministry of angels.*
4. *The continuous existence of the human soul.*
5. *Personal responsibility.*
6. *Compensation and retribution hereafter for all the good
   and evil deeds done on earth.*
7. *Eternal progress open to every human soul.*

to from the hospital; no, this was a vibrant sound, husky with a
dash of playful mirth. I pressed my lips together to keep myself
from laughing.

She was singing and dancing up and down the aisle,
celebrating her change from suffering physical presence to
limitless soul. I felt so happy for Nicki, who was free to be as
lively as she was before she got sick.

I must have looked like a cat watching a fly zip back and
forth in the air. "Nicki," I whispered, "slow down."

Shoshanna, sitting beside me, turned her head and gave me
a quizzical look.

One of Nicki's daughters got up to speak. There was a
noticeable pressure change in the air as Nicki's energetic
performance came to a full stop and she listened to her daughter
tearfully remember her childhood. At the end of her eulogy, she
wiped her eyes, looked up and said, "I love you, Mom," and then
threw a kiss into the air.

In my ear, Nicki whispered, "Leah, honey, I'm here."

The service ended and people stood up to go. I felt Nicki's
sadness that her friends and family were leaving. I felt sad, too,
because I knew our little circle of support was breaking up. We

hugged each other and wished each other well. One woman said, "What a beautiful service. If only Nicki could've been here to see it." I smiled knowingly.

As Shoshanna and I walked back to our cars, she thanked me again for being part of the group. I said I was honoured, then added, "Nicki was distracting me during the service, running all over the place."

Shoshanna chuckled. "Y'know, I felt something in there, too."

∘ ∘
∘ ∘

Chapter 7

A Private Matter

∘ ∘
∘ ∘

No matter how hard I tried, I could not give the young woman a message. And yet, deep down, spirit was telling me not to leave the woman alone. And, later, after I finally talked with her, I understand why it seemed like she had been enveloped in an impenetrable cloak.

This happened at one of the first public message events that I organized, in a small room above a New Age bookstore north of Toronto. I was excited to try out a new method of message delivery I had just learned from medium Sharon Klingler. Sharon's method is called "spirit-centred"; using this technique, I listened to spirit and let them steer me where they wanted. Before, I had used a more "client-centred" technique, where I would ask an individual in the audience, "May I come to you?"

then proceed to tune into that person's vibration and give that individual a message. The main difference between these two techniques is that with spirit-centred, I would describe the image of a spirit person who wanted to speak because I was with that spirit, and then wait for a member of the audience to claim the presence. (At one time, Canadian Spiritualist churches preferred the "client-centred" method during services, but more and more congregations are accepting mediums who practice "spirit-centred" mediumship.)

Approximately twenty people had come to see me deliver messages from spirit, and since the number seemed manageable, I decided I would give a mediumistic message to everyone in attendance. As the evening wound down, I realized I had brought through spirits for just about everyone — except one young woman sitting in the centre of the room. I switched to the client-centred method, and that is when I hit a psychic roadblock.

I looked into her eager eyes and concentrated hard for a few moments. Nothing. All I saw were her round, brown eyes, and the hopeful look on her face. Clearly, she was yearning to hear from someone, and I wanted so badly to bring her spirit person in to her. But ...

Nothing.

Okay, guys, I mentally told my guides, *round two.*

I asked the woman for her name. Often, hearing a name is like putting a key into a lock that opens a person's soul. Plus, when she spoke I would hear her voice, which would also help me tune into her vibration.

"Lucille," she said shyly.

I focused on her voice and closed my eyes. An image began to form in my mind. *Thank you*, I told my guides, then said, "A man is coming in for you." *Why had Lucille at first seemed so hard to read?* "Spirit is showing me a man digging through the dirt for worms. He's a fisherman, and he used to go worm hunting at sunrise. And sometimes, he made a big joke of it."

Lucille's expression went from expectant to puzzled. Her reaction surprised me, and I wondered if I had brought through someone Lucille had not wanted to hear from. Then I saw that the middle-aged woman sitting behind Lucille was waving her arm excitedly.

"That's my dad," the woman crowed.

I turned my attention to her and said the smiling fisherman was pointing to a box that smelled like fish guts. "Oh, yeah," she said with a laugh. "It wasn't just the box that stunk when he got home from his little fishing trips. He just thought that was such a hoot."

The crowd laughed along with her. I gave the woman a message from her father, then focused again on Lucille. It didn't take long before another male energy presented itself. "Oh, my," I said, as the image became clearer in my mind. "He's not very tall. He looks like Bruce Springsteen. Sideburns that look like they end in a point. He's wearing wraparound sunglasses. He passed from a car accident. But he's showing me a motorcycle. Two motorcycles."

Another blank look from Lucille. But a man wearing a denim jacket who was sitting two chairs away from Lucille raised his arm and nodded thoughtfully. "Sounds like my cousin," he said with a grunt. "He died when a car hit one of his Harleys."

I passed the fellow in denim a quick message from his cousin in spirit: "Keep on riding, but don't forget to check the rearview mirror." Then I looked again at Lucille, and this time moved to stand beside her chair, to get closer to her energy.

The third try was no charm: a female energy presented herself, but was quickly claimed as the grandmother of a matronly woman sitting in front of Lucille. I began wondering if Lucille was a portal — someone whose energy draws in spirits for other people. Yet … there was something about Lucille that would not let me go. I just *knew* there was something important I needed to tell her. So I said to her, "How about I speak to you after the event?"

She nodded tentatively. And for the next couple of minutes, I continued giving messages to others with no problem.

Afterward, Lucille waited patiently while several audience members approached me with questions about Spiritualism, psychic intuition, meditation, and even the stone I was wearing around my neck (zebra jasper). Then I took Lucille aside and we sat in folding chairs, facing each other. Lucille seemed relieved that it was just her and I in the room.

Suddenly, the emotional floodgates opened. An intense sadness washed over me, and this sorrow seemed to swirl around her, despite her cheerful smile. Mystified, I could not understand why, ten minutes ago, I had struggled to come up with anything, when now I was getting so much grief … so much, in fact, I had to ask my guides to turn the psychic volume down.

"The person you were hoping to hear from this afternoon," I said, speaking from my gut, "a woman … a young woman, like yourself …"

And then in my mind, I saw that woman in spirit. She had long, straight her, with bangs cut severely across her forehead. There was something haunting about her sorrowful eyes. She appeared to be Lucille's age. The spirit woman did not want to identify herself further, but gave me bits and pieces of what she was like when she was alive. And she really wanted me to understand her anguish.

"She completed suicide," I said quietly. "She seems confused, and angry. She couldn't find a way to process her anger. And … was dancing important to her?"

Tears came to Lucille's eyes. "Yes," she said. "That's her. She loved dancing. She used to dance by herself in her bedroom while she listened to her iPod."

"She says, 'Thank you for caring.' And, 'Lucy, it's not your fault.'"

"But I should've called her that night. I was supposed to call her."

I placed a comforting hand on her shoulder — or, perhaps, Lucille's friend was using me to console her. I told Lucille that her friend was trying to work things out on the other side of life. The anger she had lived with had not been directed at anyone, except herself — and that is always the hardest type of rage to deal with.

Then I assured Lucille that on the other side of the veil, when it comes to suicide, people are not judged. They review their life, then evaluate their own actions. Unfortunately, here on the Earth plane, people do judge, and often too harshly. (That is why I prefer to use the word "completed" with suicide, because saying someone "committed" the act sounds like saying that person "committed" a crime.) I then told Lucille her friend was still in the process of understanding herself and trying to go forward; the good news was she was no longer feeling emotional pain.

As Lucille thanked me and got up to leave, I realized why I had not been able to read for her earlier — spirit knew that hers was a message I should not deliver in front of others. Such is the wisdom of spirit; during the message event I did not understand my difficulty reaching Lucille, but they did. Even in a public message service or event, some things are better left private.

Chapter 8

They Come Because They Love You

The first time I heard this question, I was saddened. It happened at the end of my reading with Mika, a second-generation Canadian. Mika's mother, Keiko, had emigrated from Japan when she was sixteen because her parents had arranged a marriage with a successful businessman in Vancouver. A year after their marriage, the first of seven children were born. Keiko found it difficult to adjust to the new country, and because she did not speak English well, was reluctant to make friends. But she was loyal to her husband and a dutiful mother to their children.

On her fiftieth birthday, she was diagnosed with stage four breast cancer, and quietly passed into spirit several months later.

The reading was very evidential, but difficult, as Keiko's spirit was just as shy with me as she was when she had been living.

Plus, she had never been the kind of person who wanted to complain or bother anyone (sadly, this is why her breast cancer had remained undetected for so long). But Mika was happy to hear that her mother was watching over her two grandchildren, and occasionally visited her childhood home in Japan near Sendai, where as a child she loved to stand on a grassy hill and watch the sun rise over the Pacific Ocean.

At the end of our session, Mika seemed listless. I thought the reading had gone well, and Mika had been energized by her mother's compassionate words. Yet she was now looking unsettled. I asked her if she was all right. Mika nodded.

"Did your mother say anything that upset you?" I asked.

She sighed. "Why didn't she tell me that she loved me?"

Actually, I hear that question a lot. It happened again several months later when I brought in a husband who had passed, and I described him down to the holes in the knees of the dungarees he wore when he worked in the garden. He made his wife laugh many times, and gave her several wonderful messages about their family and friends. But when our session ended, she said she felt her husband had let her down.

I got the question again from a couple whose young son had died in the hospital, and came to tell his mother and father that his lungs no longer hurt and he was fine now. They were relieved to hear that he was no longer suffering. But …

I've even heard from pets that asked me to thank their former owners for getting them a favourite chew toy, and wanted their owners to know that they are happily waiting to play again with their beloved humans on the other side. Yet …

These readings leave clients very moved. They are overjoyed to hear from absent friends and loved ones. But for some people, evidence and encouraging words are fine; however, at the end of the session they feel as if there was one last important piece of information that I neglected to reveal. So they turn to me with disappointment in their eyes and say something like, "They didn't tell me that they still loved me."

And I reply, in a gentle voice: "They came because they love you."

That is what I told Mika. During the reading, I felt that she wanted so badly to hear this from her mother, but I cannot put words into spirit's mouth. I have never done that, and never will. As the saying goes, truth may be painful to hear but, in the end, lies are always more damaging.

In my mind's eye, I saw Mika's mother standing in the corner of the room, her eyes closed, her head slightly bowed, her small hands clasped before her as if she was in prayer. "Mika," I said, reading her mother's energy, "was your mother comfortable expressing her feelings when she was alive?"

Another gentle sigh. "No. I don't ever remember her saying, 'I love you.' I remember I kept wishing she would. She just did her mom thing." Then she grinned. "Sometimes she was so quiet, I wouldn't even know if she was in the same room."

I gently reminded Mika of that old saw: "Actions speak louder than words." It was important to Keiko to come to see her daughter, so she had willed herself into my reading room. You see, it takes a lot of effort for spirits to cross into our world and make their presence known. That is why I often tell clients that before they come, think about the person on the other side that you would like to connect with. Think of it as making a date with the spirit. Then, the spirit can focus its energy on being at a certain place at a certain time.

Of course, there are times when a spirit does not show up. It does happen — a client with a guilty conscience wants to hear from Uncle Albert because she wants to apologize to him for spreading rumours about his stinginess and his bad breath. So

I focus and focus and beg my guides to please go rustle up the fellow so my client can make her peace — but no Uncle Albert. It is the spirit world's way of saying, "Go peddle fish." Or Uncle Albert *kind of* comes through. He presents himself to me, but stands way behind me with his arms crossed over his chest and a belligerent look on his face. When this happens, the best I can do is ask my client, "Is there anyone else you would like to hear from?" And more times than not, Uncle Albert will take a few steps away, but still hang around, sticking to his guns and giving the client a silent "Nyah-nyah."

And then there are times that a spirit that the client never expected to hear from shows up. I love those moments.

I'll never forget Vic's session. It was the middle-aged man's first time seeing a medium, and he was very nervous. When he first sat down, he unbuttoned his charcoal-coloured suit jacket, and a minute later he buttoned it up again.

Vic made his appointment on the first anniversary of his mother's passing, and he was heartened when she came through very strongly. I described her as a lady of the arts, and her shoes always had to match her handbag when she went to a gala. Vic smiled at that. Later, she told Vic her presence had been with him last night at the opera, and, like him, she had enjoyed the tenor's rendition of the classic aria "Nessun Dorma." Vic wiped his eyes with a tissue. Puccini's *Turandot* had been his mother's favourite opera, and he had bought tickets for himself and his partner partly in honour of her.

But then Vic's father wanted to speak with him. Vic tensed in the chair, and his hands tightened around the arm rests. "No," he muttered, then, "I don't know." But Vic's father urged me on: *Please*, I heard him in my mind. *Please let me speak.* I told this to Vic, and he pursed his lips, then gave a quick nod and closed his eyes, as if he was afraid of what he was about to see.

When he was alive, Vic's father refused to accept his son's homosexuality, and, over his wife's protests, banished him from the house. He forbade Vic's brothers and sisters from talking with him. For the next couple years, Vic's mother and siblings had to meet him in secret. Their Christmas celebrations were anything but festive. Two years later, Vic's father died of a heart attack; his mother never remarried and died twenty-two years later.

The words came slowly. "He wants to say hello," I said. "He's calling you his son."

Vic wept silently as he listened to his father in spirit say that he had made a terrible mistake. He had not understood his son's lifestyle, and felt that Vic's choice was a blow to his own manhood. He had equated homosexuality with weakness, but now he recognized that it took a lot of courage for Vic to live with his truth, and he was proud of his son's choice. He talked of making peace with his child, and hoped it was not too late. And if Vic was okay with it, his father, a successful salesman when he was alive, would like to help Vic get his new printing business off the ground.

Vic listened to the healing message with tears in his eyes. He nodded and said in a choked whisper, "Thanks, Dad."

After the session, I gave Vic a little extra time to compose himself, and asked if he wanted to talk about what had just occurred. Vic shook his head, then said, "I've just got to think about it for awhile." He shook his head again. "I hated him. I never visited his grave. Why did he come?"

To answer his questioning look, I gently said, "He came because he loves you."

○ ○
○ ○

Chapter 9

The Ones That Get Away

○ ○
○ ○

Delivering messages from spirit is one of the most joyous things I do. It's an act of love and sharing that connects me with the spirit world, and to the recipient who is eager to hear from a departed loved one or friend. I feel that way whether I am working one-on-one with a client, or going one-on-several-dozen when I serve spirit by working at a public message event. The more the merrier, I say — except that due to time constraints I cannot touch everyone in a large crowd. This is especially true at Lily Dale, where it is not uncommon to work before a couple hundred people who are all eager to hear from someone on the other side.

After one public event, I was asked: does every spirit person I contact end up being taken by someone in the audience? I wish

I could say yes, because I know how hard spirit people work to get through the veil. But, every now and then, a spirit that presents itself to me goes as unclaimed as a child's mitten in a school's lost-and-found box. Then, what often happens is that I will get an email later from someone who had suffered from "psychic amnesia," a phrase I first heard used by medium John Edward. A person suffers from psychic amnesia when he forgets that the Bill, Mary, or Joe I had been describing was really Uncle Bill, Cousin Mary, or Joe the fraternity-buddy poker player he had not seen in decades.

Sometimes, in those cases, a spirit will work so hard to get through that it refuses to leave the room. This happened at one "Medium's Night" event I volunteered at in Cleveland, Ohio. I kept feeling a man with a military connection, and he showed me Vietnam. I could not see his face, and the other information I picked up seemed jumbled. I asked the audience if the spirit resonated with anyone, and was met with shrugs and silence. After a few moments, I blessed the spirit and moved on. But two mediums later, the speaker gestured to a heavy-set man in the third row and said, "Have you been to the Vietnam War Memorial in Washington, D.C., recently?" The man nodded, and the medium went on to deliver a message from a fellow Marine who did not come home — he had stepped on a land mine while out on patrol.

Other times, a spirit goes unclaimed because either I did not get a detail correct, or I misinterpreted what I saw. For example, I told one audience that I was feeling the presence of a man with a name that sounded like Broadbent, and he was coming to me in an Army uniform. I also felt a connection to the First World War. "Can anyone take this soldier?" I asked, scanning the room to make eye contact with as many people as possible. People made eye contact back, but no one spoke up, so I let it go. After the event, my husband heard a woman remark that she knew a Broadbent who fought in the First World War, but he had served in the Navy, not the Army.

What I find sad is when a spirit goes untaken, and then later, someone from the audience approaches to say that he was afraid to talk in front of the group, so can I give him the message now? I try, but usually once the spirit leaves me, it takes its energy with it. Is the spirit disappointed because the audience member did not want to embrace it? I have no answer for that; all I know is if the party at the other end is not able to pick up the receiver, the call is disconnected.

These are instances of lapses — "accidental refusals," I call them — not out-and-out rejections. Who would not want to get a message from a loved one in spirit? Well, believe it or not, some people *do not* want to be contacted by spirit, and even get angry at a public message event when I want to speak with them. It does not happen often, but when it occurs, I am always astounded.

A few summers ago, I worked an outdoor event on a warm afternoon. We were in a clearing within a small forest surrounded by three-hundred-year-old trees with lush green crowns. Lilac, lavender, and other sweet scents perfumed the air, which was stirred by gentle breezes. Everyone's faces were warmed by the sun. I was speaking before a crowd of just over 150 people. The vibes were good, and I was connecting well with people.

Until …

The spirit of a drummer presented himself, and I described him to the crowd. "He was in a marching band," I said, and this fellow had so much energy, I had to smile. He loved being in parades, and the attention he got when he marched down the street thumping his great big drum.

"I see him wearing something like a harness, with a big round drum balanced on his chest," I continued. "He's beating his drum: *Boom! Boom! Boom!*" I said, mimicking his forceful actions with my arms. "He's tall and has very broad shoulders. He wore horn-rimmed glasses, which he hated because he thought they made him look like a geek, but he didn't wear them when he was marching. And I'm hearing the name 'Laura' somehow associated with him. Can anyone take this fellow?"

Dead silence.

I looked around the crowd. More than 150 faces looked back at me, and none with recognition. *How could this be? I don't make this stuff up!* The drummer had presented himself so clearly. I asked the spirit to point out to me who in the crowd I should go to. Though, with people packed together so closely this afternoon, I would be happy if he directed me to the area where the person that I needed to speak with was sitting.

But the drummer had quieted. In fact, he seemed to be marching away.

And then self-doubt started creeping in. *Could I have been wrong?* I wondered. Even though I had just given two bang-on readings, even though I've been a psychic medium for more than thirty years, and trust myself and the impressions I get, it's easy to retreat into uncertainty when things don't go right.

I asked the crowd again if the drummer seemed familiar. "Don't think of family," I said. "He could've been a friend, or someone you know who might've been close to this person. You may have gone to school with him."

Uncomfortable stillness. I said a quiet prayer and blessed the spirit for coming, and then let him go. I thanked the crowd for letting me serve spirit, then walked off. As the next medium approached the platform and began to connect with the spirit world, I felt a twinge of regret that I was not able to help the drummer, who must have wanted so badly to give his love to someone.

Afterward, I was walking with my husband on a winding path through the trees when two young women stopped us. They looked to be in their late teens or early twenties. One woman, who wore ripped leggings and a sleeveless shirt, said in a cold voice, "I think that drummer was for me. But I didn't want to hear from him. And I don't want to know anything about Laura." With a flash of angry eyes and a quick toss of the head, she and her friend hurried away.

I was startled by the woman's hostility — it seemed to pulse out of her in waves. I am almost ashamed to admit it now, but the first emotion I felt was anger. *How dare she not take that spirit, and embarrass me in front of all those people?* I thought. But then I realized I had let her antagonism affect me, and blew out a few quick breaths to centre myself. And then I felt sadness, for the spirit that had tried to get through, and for this young woman who obviously still carried around a lot of pain and hurt. What had the drummer done to her? I wondered, then asked the question of my husband.

"You don't know that she's in pain," he replied. "You're only the medium. You deliver messages, not answers. And you can't make people choose to take a message."

How true. Just like some letters end up in post offices as undeliverable, some spirit will go unclaimed. And I'll always feel sad for the ones that get away.

Chapter 10

The Healing Gift

*A former classmate of mine, a respected colleague, and a well-*regarded medium in the United States, has a tumour in her pituitary gland that may be inoperable. After I received that information, I placed her name in my healing circle and meditated on her recovery. And on my next visit to my Spiritualist church, I wrote her name on a slip of paper and placed it in "the blue healing temple," which is shaped like a little church. That vessel is filled with names, and the congregation sends each person healing prayers every week.

I believe in absent healing — also called distance healing — because we have the ability to transmit our thoughts and feelings to others. It is the same principle as when you think about someone, and then she "picks up" those thoughts subconsciously, goes to the telephone and rings you up, saying she suddenly had the urge to call. Similarly, during absent healing, we send our love and healing thoughts to faraway friends — and even strangers! — with the hope that their soul accepts the energy and will be stimulated toward wellness by our prayers for their recovery.

Several years ago, I was part of a wondrous healing experience. It strengthened my belief in the power of absent healing, and deepened my trust in spirit.

I was at Cober Hill, a Spiritualist centre in England, where I had gone to hear noted English physical medium Stewart Alexander. A hundred workshop participants were eagerly awaiting Stewart's Friday night talk on the history of British Spiritualism. Stewart is in his seventies, but looks a dashing forty-five, and he has one of those animated yet regal British accents that hold listeners spellbound. Even if he had been speaking about the history of dust, I am sure I would have found the talk fascinating.

Stewart walked to the front of the room around 8:00 p.m. and looked out over the crowd. He clasped his hands before his chest, and, in a quiet voice, asked us to sit a few moments in silence and to send healing energy to three good friends of the group who had taken ill. One of them, Malcolm, had been admitted to a hospital in Milan, Italy, with pneumonia. Though I did not know it at the time, the illness was affecting Malcolm's mind, keeping him from sleeping and giving him mild hallucinations.

We sat quietly with bowed heads, and I asked the divine to let me help these people whom I had never met. I had no idea what they looked like, or even where in Milan Malcolm was located. I envisioned sending a warm, blue light out from my heart, and asked that my healing force join the collective peaceful energy of my fellow workshop attendees.

After several minutes, Stewart said, "Thank you" in a humble voice, and gave us a welcoming smile. Then he began his entertaining and informative talk, and we listened with rapt attention for the next ninety minutes.

(A side note: My husband, Benjamin, asked a question at the end of the talk and the workshop organizer said, "Oh, you must be Ben." His eyes popped as he turned to me and said, "Wow! These people are really psychic!" I laughed, not having the heart to tell him that he was the only person in the room with an American accent.)

The next evening, over a typical English dinner of boiled meat, boiled potatoes, and boiled vegetables, Stewart entered the dining room with a look of utter joy on his face. He had just heard from Malcolm's wife, Edith, and had an incredible story to tell.

"Yesterday evening, as Malcolm lay on his bed, with his wife sitting beside him," Stewart said, "he suddenly felt completely enveloped by a peaceful energy, and he quickly slipped into a deep, healing sleep." It was, Stewart added, the first time Malcolm had felt comfortable in days.

While I was glad to hear the good news, I had to wonder: was the easing of Malcolm's illness due to absent healing? The Italian hospital was located thousands of miles from Cober Hill, and I was a tad skeptical of the veracity of the experience. I later wrote Stewart about my feelings, and received this reply from Edith:

> Malcolm had been confused/semi-lucid for five days when we got him into hospital and, at times, he wasn't making a great deal of sense. He couldn't always remember where he was and occasionally was seeing things. On Friday evening, he was sitting out of bed when he suddenly announced, "I have to get into bed."

He did so and lay down. I stood at the foot
of the bed and suddenly sensed a wonderful,
warm energy. I said, "I think they're doing a
healing." I checked the time; it was about 8:10
p.m. Malcolm said, "The energy is huge" and
easily went to sleep. I stayed for about another
half hour, then drove home and rang Stewart to
ask if there had been any healing thoughts sent.
He confirmed it; the healing would have been
just about ten past eight.

On Saturday morning, I found Malcolm so
much better. All the confusion had gone and
did not return.

I finally met Malcolm two years later. The pneumonia had
definitely slowed down the spry octogenarian, but he was in
good spirits and looking forward to his next trip to Italy.

I would like to think that my hopeful thoughts for a speedy
recovery helped Malcolm get back on his feet. Prayer is a
wondrous thing — if nothing else, it sends positive energy into
the atmosphere. And when it comes to cleaning the psychic air,
every little bit of optimistic thought helps.

And so I have also added the name of my fellow psychic
from the States to the blue healing temple at my Spiritualist
church, The Church of Universal Love, in Toronto. Now, we
hope for the best.

I also keep my colleague's name on my own personal prayer
list, which is Scotch-taped to my desk blotter, and send a blessing
every time my eyes alight on her name. When you practise
healing, you spread hope. And when you pray for the health of
others, you are also strengthening the love within yourself.

Chapter 11

My Father-in-Law's Grave

° °
° °

After I finished the reading, my client and I began talking and joking about our husbands. We agreed that a woman did not have to be psychic to know who was responsible for the pile of dirty clothes in the corner of the bedroom, and how often our hubbies have offered to wash the dishes. (If your number is higher than zero, ladies, please email me your secret.)

As I walked my client out of my office, she said, "Your husband is lucky. You can give him readings whenever he wants, and bring him his relatives who have crossed over all the time."

I just smiled to myself. Yes, of course my husband, Benjamin, is lucky to have me! But, no, he never asks me for readings. I have never volunteered to connect him with someone who has passed. And I never will.

I do not force on my husband any psychic or mediumistic impressions, for the same reason I do not approach strangers on the street or in the supermarket when one of their loved ones suddenly pops into my inner radar with a message. I honour people's privacy. After all, maybe the young woman pushing the shopping cart down the frozen food aisle does not want to hear from nosy-but-departed Aunt Lucy. And what right do I have to tell the overweight East Indian man scanning the chocolate ice cream on sale that his mother in spirit wants him to start losing weight?

Another reason I shy away from giving messages to my family and close friends is that it's difficult to be objective with people you know really well. Ego keeps getting in the way, which means there is too much attachment to the outcome. Because you care about someone, you naturally want any message to be good, so there is a tendency to paint a rosy picture even though storm clouds are gathering on the horizon — and that person may really need to know about the threat of those clouds.

There is nothing stormy about my relationship with Benjamin, outside the fact that he is a Leo and I am a Taurus. Benjamin is my second husband, which meant there was a bit of a challenge for both of us getting to know new family members, and integrating his kinfolk with mine. Family means a lot to me and, thankfully, things have gone pretty smoothly. But there is something missing in our relationship, and when we were courting I really felt it. Days before my father passed, Benjamin asked my dad for his blessing on our marriage. But I never had the chance to do the same. I wish I could have met my husband's father.

• • •

Benjamin's father died from a brain aneurysm ten years before we married. But I have learned from experiences with my clients that parents will always be parents, and they will always be concerned and interested in our welfare, whether they are living across town or living in spirit.

About a month after my father passed, he came to me to say hi — but I was in the bathroom at the time. I almost screamed when I heard his deep voice: "Hello, Carolyn."

Maybe I did scream. "Dad, what are you doing? I'm taking a shower!"

"Oh, sorry, sorry," he said, and I felt his energy withdraw. (Spirit people are attracted to our inner light, so they are not always aware of what the body housing that light is doing.)

A few minutes later, after I had finished dressing, I heard his voice again, and we had a short, pleasant conversation.

I have never met my husband's father in the flesh. But I have felt his presence on occasion. The first time, I sensed a tall, studious man, and there was some kind of association with numbers. (Benjamin's father was a math teacher.) I heard the word "father" and my husband's face popped into my mind, and I thought, *aha*. Since then, he has always identified himself the same way. On several of those instances I remarked to my husband, "Your father's here." The statement was usually met with an utterance like "Oh?" or a half-hearted nod, and then dismissed. A couple times, my father-in-law and I exchanged pleasantries, but I did not pass our conversations on to his son, because I was not sure if he wanted to hear them.

I enjoy the warm glow my father-in-law presents when he draws close. I am sure he likes me: in fact, he showed up in a reading Benjamin received in Lily Dale, New York, from the charming Patricia Price. Pat did not know my husband or what I did for a living when she told my fiancé (at the time), chuckling, "Your father is here, and he's glad that you've found a happy medium."

I know he was at our wedding. And whenever we drove to Columbus, Ohio, to visit my mother-in-law and the rest of my husband's family, I felt him, too. My brother-in-law has dreamed about him regularly, so I know there is contact. Yet when I would tell my husband that his father's spirit was near, he reacted coolly, then stayed silent.

I regarded my husband with curiosity during those times and wondered why he acted so unmoved whenever his father was around. What was their relationship like? What transpired between them to give me the strong impression that there was some kind of unfinished business that needs to be taken care of?

But as much as I cared about my husband's state of emotions, I would not trespass into any private corners of his mind.

So I was a little surprised when my husband announced that on the next trip to his hometown of Cleveland, Ohio, to visit his daughter and our friends, he wanted to visit his father's grave — something he had not done since his father was buried twelve years prior.

The day he chose for the visit was perfect. The cemetery was quiet that morning, and crisp, gentle breezes stirred the treetops. My husband grew quiet and focused as he steered the car through the wrought-iron gate and we entered the grounds. After a quick stop at the groundskeeper's office to get directions, he drove slowly over the winding road that took us deeper into the graveyard. Gravel crunched under the tires.

Row upon row of granite and marble headstones gleamed in the late-morning light. Each grave marker held a name, and behind each name was a story that wanted to be remembered by someone in the living. I felt the presence of spirit, as I do whenever I visit a graveyard, yet today the storytellers seemed respectfully still.

This was a Jewish cemetery. We passed a black marble obelisk that towered over a flat, black stone buried in the ground.

A waist-high black marble barrier circled this monument, and hundreds of names were etched in white around the circle. I was captivated by the frightening beauty of that monument. It was a Holocaust memorial, and driving by the shrine, I was seized with such sadness I wanted to weep. Yet I could not look away, for I felt that here were spirits that wanted to be noticed and remembered, even though their passing was tragic. I said a quick prayer and blessed them, and I felt them thank me for thinking of them.

Benjamin located his father's gravestone and stopped the car. The polished white marker was simple, bearing my father-in-law's name and years of his birth and passing — the simple facts of a life well lived. The grave itself was well tended, with lush, green grass that had been carefully trimmed. It was truly a resting place.

Leaving the car, I accompanied him to the site. I felt like saying something to this man whom I had never met in the flesh, but I realized that this was the time for my husband to be alone with his dad. A few moments went by as my husband stood still. I could not read his expression. He looked at the headstone and then down at his hands, and I stopped myself from trying to understand what was going through his head.

Then he grimaced.

"I forgot the rock I wanted to bring," he said. He had found the greenish stone last month, when we had taken a walk along a Lake Ontario beach, and he had wanted to bring it because it represented his new home in Canada. It is a Jewish custom to leave a small rock — a piece of eternal earth — on a gravestone as a sign of remembrance. You are telling the spirit, *I was here.*

"How about if I leave a toonie?" he asked. "That'll be like leaving him a piece of Canada."

I told him that was a fine idea.

I gave my husband a quick hug and a smile, and then walked back to the car.

I purposely looked away while my husband stood at his father's grave. Time passed. I do not know what was said between his father and him, but I am sure they talked. Perhaps there were tears. I closed my eyes, leaned toward the windshield, and felt the warm sun on my face. When my husband returned to the car he was silent, but I felt something had changed. I did not ask anything of him and did not try to contact his father, but I suddenly received the mental image of a wound that was healing. I thanked my guides for this image, and then asked them to respect my husband's privacy.

○ ○
○ ○

Chapter 12

Three Seconds of Terror

○ ○
○ ○

Whenever I walk down the aisle to stand in front of several
hundred people and deliver messages from spirit, I recall my
husband's definition of public mediumship: "Three seconds of
terror, followed by five minutes of bliss."

I used to be terrified of speaking in public, but no more.
Now I look forward to working public message services every
summer in Lily Dale, New York. For mediums, it is a great
honour to serve spirit and humanity at Lily Dale, and bring
loving messages from the afterlife to random audience members.

But my husband's words came back to me the day I sat in a
back row bench at the Forest Temple, one of the three gathering
places in Lily Dale where public message events occur. Forest
Temple, with its Doric columns, resembles a cross between a

small Roman temple and an outdoor theatre. It is located at the edge of a forest and faces dozens of benches.

That summer afternoon, the benches were quickly filling with people eager to receive a message from spirit. Sitting toward the back of the gathering, I spied a young woman two benches to the left of me. A purple scrunchy held her ponytail, and her corduroy overalls were worn at the knees. Her eyes were closed and she gently rubbed her palms together while taking slow, deep breaths.

I moved to the back of the audience to chat with the medium who was chairing the service. She told me the young woman was a student of a respected Lily Dale medium and teacher, and she was centering herself to prepare to deliver her first public message.

I watched the student medium trying to meditate away her jitters and sent her encouraging energy. *I was once you*, I thought, as I remembered that afternoon in 2003 when I, too, screwed up my courage and delivered my first message in front of more than two hundred people in Lily Dale. *Me, and every other medium who has ever stood at the edge of our confidence, and leaped off into space with nothing in our parachute pack except faith.*

(I have heard it said that the fear of public speaking is even greater than our fear of death — in other words, we would rather be lying in the coffin than delivering the eulogy.)

● ● ●

But first, let me briefly describe Lily Dale, the largest Spiritualist community in North America and one of my favourite spots in the world. Believers in the afterlife and those who are not sure what they believe have been visiting this gated village since it was founded in 1879. Some of its more famous guests have been Sir Arthur Conan Doyle, Susan B. Anthony, and Mae West.

For nine weeks every summer, Lily Dale (*www.lilydaleassembly.com*) offers visitors intriguing programs that run the gamut from spiritual to philosophical, and from fun to woo-woo. Just about every season opens with a presentation by the Tibetan Buddhist Monks of the Drepung Loseling Monastery, who lead chanting and meditation services and create a marvellous sand Mandela. Wayne Dyer, Deepak Chopra, and Jason Hawes and Grant Wilson (paranormal investigators from the television show *The Ghost Hunters*) have lectured here. I have taught several psychic development and mediumship workshops here, and am grateful every time I am asked to be a presenter.

Lily Dale is home to many registered mediums, spiritual healers, and other Spiritualists, but not everyone lives in the village year-round. The community, located on the shore of Lake Cassadaga, lies in the heart of the heart of the snowbelt. In winter, snowfall is measured in metres and a common sight is rooftop icicles that touch the ground. But during summer months, when the residential population triples to about seven hundred and the centuries-old trees show off their lush green crowns, walking through the village is a delight.

The sixteen streets are narrow (how do they fit in the snow plows?) and no two houses are alike. A boxy but quaint bungalow sits beside a grand Victorian home with turrets and bay windows. On the next street, a white clapboard house that needs a new coat of paint is next to an immaculate Cape Cod, while farther down the block is the kind of place the Keebler elves would go to after a long day of baking cookies in a tree. And cats are everywhere: big, fluffy felines in all colours that lie in the sun and cast don't-you-dare-ignore-me looks if you do not stop to pet them.

I especially enjoy Lily Dale just after sunrise, as the morning haze is lifting off the lake, and the grassy, rolling hills on the other side of the shore are painted with mist. The air smells small-town fresh. Some mornings, a family of trumpeter swans leads their cygnets across the water. But if you stroll along the lakeshore to the beach, tread the sand carefully — Canadian geese leave their own kind of messages.

For history buffs, the Marion Skidmore Library houses hundreds of volumes on Spiritualism and other esoteric topics, with many of the tomes dating from the 1800s. The Lily Dale Museum is crammed with antiques and artifacts relating to the birth of Spiritualism, women's suffrage, and Lilydaliana. Plus, there is a collection of slate drawings, spirit paintings, and incredible photographs of physical mediums using ectoplasm to create amazing phenomena.

The Maplewood Hotel, a rebuilt horse barn, hasn't changed much since it opened a century ago. Gossips swear the place is haunted; stories abound of horse whinnies in the middle of the night, and a lady in Victorian clothes who floats up the second-floor stairway. When booking accommodations, people often request a haunted room, but the staff politely says that the rooms are as clear as a minister's conscience.

But Lily Dale's main attractions are the three daily public message services (four if you count the shorter divine service held every afternoon in the Lily Dale Auditorium), where mediums from around the world volunteer to serve spirit. At the major message services, mediums are given the opportunity to deliver three messages in about five minutes (long-winded mediums usually give two messages) before crowds that often number in the hundreds. Of the three daily message events, one is held at the Forest Temple, while the other two are at Inspiration Stump.

"The Stump" is a huge, concrete-topped hemlock stump located in a clearing in the Leolyn Woods, a section of virgin forest at the south end of the village. Like the Forest Temple, the Stump faces several dozen benches. I love giving messages at the Stump, where I feel Lily Dale's positive energy is the greatest. Interestingly, in 1898 (or 1902, depending on who you talk to) Canadian mediums were the first group to give public messages at the Stump, which was at that time called "the meeting in the Woods." In honour of that, Lily Dale hosts Canadian Weekend over the civic holiday in the first weekend of August. During that time, visitors can see Canadian mediums and healers, and join in an ol'-fashioned singalong.

Fun fact: John Edward got the idea for his TV show *Crossing Over* after guesting at the Stump.

There are also two daily healing services held at the Healing Temple, a rectangular building that's as plain as a good night's sleep. Inside the temple, soothing music plays in the background while white-shirted spiritual healers, their heads bowed, move their hands around the person's body in a kind of touchless massage whose aim is to fill people's souls with a sense of peace.

I had been visiting Lily Dale for several years as a spectator, not a participant, when I learned that my grandparents used to go there in the early 1940s. A cousin of mine swears there is a picture of them somewhere on the grounds, but no one can find it. I wish I had the photo; I would love to frame it on the wall in my reading room. So that every time I was curious about where I received my psychic genes, I could look at them in "The Dale" and re-experience the peace and quiet of a place where life seems to move at the speed of a cloud. And I hope that every time I walked up the aisle between benches to work at the Forest Temple or the Stump, they would watch me from the other side of the veil and be proud of me.

• • •

So there I was in 2003, more nervous than I was on my first date in high school, as I stood in the back of the Leolyn Woods clearing and told the medium chairing that afternoon's message service that I wanted to work. She looked me up and down, thanked me with a nod, and then penciled my name into her roster.

I did it because I wanted to challenge myself. I also wanted to thank spirit for supporting me through life. Because, after all, isn't that what message work is all about — giving service by helping people heal their grief by bringing them evidence that their loved ones are still with them?

And so I sat there, sweating bullets and feeling my heart hammering in my chest, waiting for my name to be called.

I closed my eyes to centre myself, prayed to my guides for help. *I can do this*, I told myself. *What's the worst that could happen?* Then I imagined the worst that could happen, and my heart pounded even faster.

Suddenly, I heard a voice — something between a heavenly sigh and a proclamation of doom:

"Our next medium is a visiting medium from Toronto: Carolyn Molnar."

It took a moment to register that the chairman of the message service had called me. ME! I swallowed hard — a softball was stuck in my throat. My lungs were lead weights as I unsteadily rose to my feet and walked down the gravel path toward the Stump. I passed benches and benches filled with people, and felt hundreds of pairs of eyes boring into my back.

I stood before the Stump and stared out at the sea of faces. In my head, I said another silent prayer, then whispered, "C'mon guys."

Time stopped.

Oh, no! I thought. *I'm not getting anything! Help!*

Then I felt like I had tunnel vision, and my eyes honed in on a woman in the fourth row who was imploring me with her eyes. I knew I needed to speak with her.

"The lady in the blue shirt," I heard myself saying — stammering? "May I come to you?"

"Yes," she said excitedly.

Once I started talking, my fear melted like warm butter. Words just seemed to flow. I had opened the floodgates, and spirit carried me. Energized, I did not want to stop talking. I do not remember what I told that woman, but she seemed pleased. And then I went to another person in the audience. More words came. I could have talked for another hour.

Unfortunately, I do not remember that message either, but the chairman of the service smiled and thanked me as I walked back to my seat.

Flash forward to true confession time!

I still get a little nervous before I do public message work, but I do not stay skittish long. I felt like telling that to the student medium who was readying herself to deliver her first public message. Then I glanced around at all the other wonderful Lily Dale mediums who have, collectively, eons of experience. I bet my fellow Canadian (and registered) mediums John White, Lynne Forget, and Debra Boardman — as well as every one of the very talented American mediums at Lily Dale — has his or her own story of first-message stress.

Fly, I want to tell the young woman in front of me. *Close your eyes and take that leap of faith. Spirit will guide you.*

And later that afternoon, she nervously delivered her message, then hurried back to her seat. I sidled over to her and told her she did a good job. "Really?" she said, with wide-eyed surprise, and I hoped she would remember this day when, sometime in the future, she will have the chance to encourage another young medium. I wonder if she will look at that youngster and see herself.

Chapter 13

Environmental Messages

One of the most interesting messages I ever delivered came through a leaf. That's right — a leaf!

It happened at an outdoor public message service at Inspiration Stump. It was a perfect August afternoon: not too hot, not too breezy, and not too many mosquitoes. Sunlight slanted through the treetops, and many people in the audience sported sunglasses.

About 250 people sat on wooden benches, listening to the medium before me, and while I waited for my name to be called, I glanced down. My gaze focused on a green maple leaf lying by itself on the hard-packed dirt. A moment of dizziness overwhelmed me, but I could not take my eyes off that leaf. What did it mean?

Somehow, I heard my name. Shaking off my light-headedness, I walked through the crowd to the front of the clearing, then turned to face the expectant crowd. So many people were hoping to get a message — who to go to first? I smiled, though on the inside I still felt a little rattled. I put the leaf out of my mind and concentrated on connecting with spirit. *Who wants to come through?* I asked my guides, then picked up a presence, and began talking. I do not remember now who I went to or what I said. All I recall is that in the back of my mind, like the last party guest who refuses to go home, was the feeling that the maple leaf was very important.

I was about to go to my second message when that leaf seemed to grow into the size of a flag and wrap itself around my head. *Ok*, I thought, *let's go with it*, and prayed that I would not sound too silly.

"I have a leaf," I said to the sea of faces. "Can anyone take a leaf?"

No reaction from anyone. *Uh-oh....*

I looked around at the trees and said, "Oh, it belongs to one of you guys?" That got a laugh from the crowd, but I was beginning to wonder if my train of thought had jumped the tracks. *A leaf!*

Trust, I felt, as if someone was whispering in my ear. *Go with it.*

So I closed my eyes for a moment to centre myself and concentrated on a picture of a maple leaf. Quickly, I began feeling more information coming through.

"This is a gentleman who liked being outside," I said, then looked over the crowd. "I'm hearing father and husband. Have you ever heard the expression, 'Going to the shed?' In England, some men have little sheds in their back yards where they like to go for a little bit of quiet time. Maybe they just go there for a cigarette, or to read the paper —"

An arm shot up in the audience. A dark-haired woman in a yellow sundress looked ready to jump to her feet. Beside the woman, two little girls were squirming and laughing.

"I think you're describing my dad," the woman said with a chuckle. "In the house that I grew up in, there was a little shed in our backyard where he used to go to smoke —"

"Tell her about the leaf!" one of her children squealed, bouncing in her seat and laughing.

"Yes," the woman said. "As we were walking here, I said to my children, 'I hope we get to hear from grandpa today.' And just as I said that, a leaf dropped on my head."

"And here it is!" cried one girl, holding it up.

There were several sighs and gasps in the crowd, and then everyone had a good laugh as the girl waved her leaf like a flag. I connected very strongly with the gentleman in spirit, and told the woman, "Your father ... he says he was a teacher. He used to read to you at night? And he shaved off his beard because it scratched your cheek when you kissed him good night?"

The woman nodded enthusiastically after each bit of evidence. "But he kept his mustache," she said with a giggle.

"Your father comes to you and your children with lots of love. He wants you to keep that leaf, and he hopes that every time you look at it, you will think of him and remember that he'll always be with you."

"We'll keep it, for sure!" one of the little girls said. Her mother smiled and wiped her eyes.

Now, who would have thought that one little leaf could hold so much meaning for someone? Or, better yet, isn't it amazing how spirit communicates to us?

While many of us "feel" spirit through our intuition — our sixth sense — spirit can also touch in with us through the world itself. This is what I call an environmental message. Spirit use their energy to get us to notice things around us that have special meaning, like a book we are inexplicable drawn to (and turns out to be just the thing we need to read to help solve a problem), or we are thinking about a certain person and their favourite song comes on the radio.

Another time when I was working at the Stump, I paused between messages and gazed up into the trees just as a light wind was rustling the foliage. For a moment, the swaying leaves looked like a field of butterflies in the air. Mesmerized, I stood with my mouth hanging open as I saw a bright blue sky filled with beautiful monarch butterflies. A blink of the eye later, I was staring at waving leaves.

So, I went with it, recounting the scene of butterflies spirit had shown me. "I feel this sight was an important memory for you," I told the audience. "I believe you were with your father that day." And I described the man I was seeing: tall and lanky, with big hands that were calloused from farm work. He was a deeply spiritual man who had a great respect for nature. In fact, he planted special bushes around his property because he knew they attracted butterflies.

A grey-haired lady raised her hand and took the spirit. It was her father, she said. She recalled the scene of butterflies; it had happened over seventy years ago, when she was five years old, and she had thought it was magical the way brightly coloured butterfly wings had suddenly filled the air like pieces of glittering stained glass.

Later, after the service, the woman sought me out and told me she had not thought about those butterflies in decades — yet the moment I started talking about them, she remembered the scene as if it had happened an hour ago. She remembered looking up at her father, who watched, enraptured, as the butterflies danced into the sky. "Are you crying, Daddy?" she had asked. Her father looked down at her and smiled, then gently placed one of his big hands on her head and tousled her hair.

The woman gave me a hug and thanked me for giving her back that memory. "Don't thank me," I said. "Thank your dad. He remembers it, too."

• • •

My husband has just told me about his favourite environmental message. He was driving on a freeway in the United States one night and saw a big neon sign mounted on poles so you could see it from a miles away. It was advertising a SUNOCO gasoline station. All of the letters had burned out, except the middle two: NO. He laughed at that. The environmental message was not for him, but he knew that someone driving that night, someone who was angry or hurt or confused, and probably facing a great decision — perhaps even a life-or-death situation — had a burning question that needed an answer. Should I leave my spouse? Am I really a failure? Should I end it all?

NO.

Let's hope, emboldened by this seemingly random message — from God's mind to your eyes, as the saying somewhat goes — that the person with a problem realized he or she is not alone in the universe, and there was a greater power to call on for help.

○ ○
○ ○

Chapter 14

The Mystery of Room 6

○ ○
○ ○

Judy, the perky manager of the Maplewood Hotel in Lily Dale, New York, smiles knowingly when you ask her about rooms that are supposedly haunted. Haunted hotel rooms are one of those Lily Dale legends that have grown by leaps and bounds over the years. Guests who sit in the rocking chairs on the Maplewood's front porch swap these tales like baseball cards, then add their own take on what they had seen or heard during their stay. If you listen to these stories long enough, you might start thinking that the Maplewood is like the Overlook Hotel, which is the centrepiece of Stephen King's novel *The Shining.*

Judy cannot count the number of times people have called for reservations and asked to stay in a haunted room. These requests are met with a feigned giggle, and the assurance that there is nothing significantly paranormal about any of the rooms. Privately, though, she admits that some guests in Rooms 6, 17, 25, 42, and 46 have occasionally reported "activity." Yet even in those rooms, weeks will often go by without anyone saying that something eerie had happened to them. In fact, more guests seem disappointed when they check out, because nothing spooktacular took place. No rattling of chains or filmy phantasms flitting across the room. Not even a mournful sigh heard in the middle of the night.

But that was not the case for us when we stayed in Room 6 and experienced paranormal activity we will never forget.

My husband loves Room 6 because it is a corner room with cross ventilation, thanks to windows on two walls. The square-shaped Maplewood Hotel was built in the 1880s, and most of the boxy rooms have a window or two on just one wall. The rooms can get quite hot in the summer (bring a fan).

Room 6 has a shower stall (not all rooms have showers or claw-foot bathtubs), a sink, and homey 1940s-type paintings gracing the walls. All rooms have a chair or two for when company drops by, and old-fashioned wooden dressers that smell like your grandma's armoire when you open the drawers.

The bad news about Room 6 is there is no closet. For my husband, a guy who was used to throwing his clothes on the floor after he wore them, that was no problem. Thankfully, I was able to get a clothes rack from the hotel staff, because I do not like to throw my clothes on the floor.

The first time we stayed together in Lily Dale, Benjamin got us that room, figuring we would enjoy cool breezes and restful July nights. And the first couple of sleeps in Room 6 were very enjoyable. But then we met Benjamin's friend, Tammy, who has been visiting Lily Dale longer than we have and has friends throughout the community. Tammy, a college professor, has the kind of long, thick straight hair that I wish I had been blessed with. She also loves to laugh and knows more stories than Scheherazade.

We were chatting with Tammy over tea and desserts at Cup-a-Joe's Coffee Shop when she asked us where we were staying. Then she asked us in which room.

Her eyebrows raised. "Oh?" she said, intrigued. "You're in there? Anything happen to you yet?"

I stopped eating my blueberry coffee cake mid-chew.

Benjamin asked, "What do you mean?"

"Well, you know, Lily Dale has had its ups and downs," Tammy said. Which was true; Lily Dale has had some questionable periods in its history, such as when Spiritualism was on the wane and undesirable elements visited the area. During Prohibition, for example, some came looking for bootleg spirits.

"At one time," Tammy continued, "what's now Room 6 was two rooms, and one of those rooms was used for poker games. Things got pretty nasty at some of those games, I've heard. There were some fights and stuff, and some pretty bad injuries."

Had either Benjamin or I been in our left brains, one of us would have asked Tammy, "How do you know this?" Instead, we swallowed her tale with eyes agog and felt thrilled to be privy to another story of the secret underbelly of Lily Dale's past.

Later, as my husband and I walked back to our room, he confessed that he had never experienced anything unworldly in the six years he had stayed in Room 6. I laughed and said, "You sound disappointed."

Be careful what you wish for, because you just might get it!

That night, I woke with a start. Something cold had brushed my back — something much colder and heavier than a breeze. My senses sharpened and I looked around the dark room. The air was still, and the silence felt deep. The fuzzy numbers on the digital clock glowed green. Warily, I put my head back on the pillow and closed my eyes.

I screamed when the cold hand again traced its fingers down my back. My husband jerked awake, sat up. "Something touched me," I whimpered, frightened. My husband, moved closer to calm me. The window shades hung flat over the open windows; there had been no breeze. I pulled the bedcovers up to our necks and shivered.

Somehow, we fell back to sleep.

The next morning, Benjamin had his own creepy story to tell. Sleeping on his back, he had suddenly awakened, feeling like a great weight was crushing his chest. He could not breathe, and turned his head toward me — yet he did not see me! It was as if I had somehow vanished! Gasping for air, he whispered a quick prayer for protection … and that was all he could remember.

We skipped the morning meditation, feeling too jittery for inner contemplation, and talked about our experiences over tea at Cup-a-Joe's. Had we really experienced something mystical, or had our minds played tricks on us? After all, our nights had been uneventful until Tammy had rattled us with her story about high-stakes poker and violent goings-on. But we had heard so many odd stories like that before — about Lily Dale and the Maplewood — why should that one have affected us?

The Maplewood is a reconditioned horse barn, and people have talked of hearing horses whinny in the middle of a night, or sounds of galloping. Then there is the legend of the ghost of a lady in a brown Victorian dress that has been seen walking up the stairs to the third floor, where she seems to melt into the air.

Lily Dale is full of ghost stories. Every week, one of the mediums leads a midnight ghost walk, and visitors bring thermometers, energy readers, night-vision goggles, cameras, and other ghost-hunting accoutrements in an effort to capture orbs (spirit energy) on film. On these walks, some people claimed to have heard animal sounds and shadowy movements in the pet cemetery. Others love to visit the Stump at midnight, because they say the energy is strongest at that time for feeling the presence of spirit. And why not? Mediums have been contacting the spirit world at the Stump for over a hundred years, so think of all the energy that has built up there over time!

My husband and I debated these questions: Is Lily Dale a magnet for the paranormal? Or was our desire to have an otherworldly experience so great that our mind (with a little nudging from Tammy) created one? And, whatever the case, shouldn't we have been thrilled with our paranormal encounter?

Well, not when we are trying to sleep, we agreed.

Besides, there is nothing to fear from spirit.

But just to be on the safe side, you can bet we said a prayer for protection and white-lighted the bed every night before we went to sleep. Thankfully, nothing else eventful happened to us during the rest of our weeklong stay.

And we never asked for Room 6 again. Until several years later ...

Due to some last-minute plans, we needed a room and 6 was available. The memory of our ghostly night seemed too distant to worry about. Besides, 6 was one of the biggest rooms in the hotel, and we were tired of staying in cramped quarters. (Being a Taurus means that when I travel, I bring as much of my home with me as I can.)

Our first night in Room 6 was cool and pleasant, and we drifted easily into sleep. Until we were awakened by the people above us, who had decided to rearrange the dresser and bed in their room at around 2:30 in the morning. And we heard muffled voices, as if some major discussion was going on. Exasperated, we looked at the ceiling, then at each other and sighed, and closed our eyes. Welcome to Lily Dale, where kooky people often do kooky things at kooky times.

We slept well the next night, and perhaps the next after that. But at some point later in the week, we woke again to the thudding sounds of the people above us dragging heavy things across their floor. Finally, my husband angrily leapt from bed, stormed into the hall and went upstairs. The sounds stopped, and I imagined him telling off our upstairs neighbours. (He's a Leo, and not afraid to roar.)

But when he came back to bed, he was quiet. "I went upstairs," he said sheepishly, "and I stood outside their door, but I didn't hear anything. I even put my ear to their door." He shrugged. "Nothing."

Next morning, we told Judy about the noises. "I don't know what it is," she said with a grin. "A couple people have said they heard what sounded like workmen clunking furniture around. But I can tell you, nobody's doing anything that late at night."

The next night, and the night after that, we heard the phantom furniture movers. And it always happened around 2:30 a.m. When the thumping started, my husband and I exchanged knowing smiles, then tried drifting back to sleep. Whoever or whatever is moving things across the floor, God bless them — but could they please do it at 2:30 p.m., when no one is trying to get some rest? *Welcome to Lily Dale*, I thought. *If you don't find spirit here, they will find you.*

Chapter 15

Proof of Spirit?

On clear, cool nights in Lily Dale, my husband and I like to grab our digital camera and go spirit hunting. Not ghost hunting, mind you, but spirit tracking.

Not that either of us wouldn't love to get a photograph of a ghost, but among those in the know, a picture of a full materialization is considered to be the Holy Grail of ghost hunting. However, it is more possible to snap photos of orbs — spheres of spirit light — for two reasons: it is easier for spirit to present themselves in the shape of a circle, and there is something about the electronics in a digital camera that seems to mesh well with spirit energy, which is a form of electricity. We know people who had been shooting cemeteries, abandoned buildings, and other such sites on film for years and have never caught anything. But the moment they switched to a digital camera or started carrying a digital video recorder — WHAM! They captured magnificent-looking orbs left and right.

There is still a lot of controversy about whether orbs are film processing errors (highly unlikely on digital camera, where there is no film), pieces of dust caught by the camera flash (dust specks photograph as uneven splotches; orbs are perfectly round circles) or moisture particles in the air (ditto). *The Orb Project*, by Dr. Klaus Heinemann, a materials science researcher at NASA, and Miceál Ledwith, the former president of Maynooth College in Ireland, is a fascinating book on this subject. The authors have researched orbs for years and amassed more than one hundred thousand images of these objects, and they believe that the light circles are emanations of spirit beings.

Benjamin and I have seen some incredible orb photographs taken by friends and fellow mediums. Some orbs appear as big as basketballs, and if you look closely at them, you can see what looks like the fuzzy outline of faces. Other orbs seem to glow a soft blue, or are coloured yellow or red.

The first time we captured spirit activity on a photograph, I was overjoyed. It happened at a public message event several years ago. Benjamin always takes a digital camera to my workshops and message events to see if we can capture orbs, ectoplasm, or any other signposts of spirit. At message events, whenever I feel drawn to an audience member and start speaking to him or her, he pulls out the trusty palm-sized camera and snaps a few images quietly and unobtrusively. (I have to take his word for that — I am usually in the zone and only aware of the person I am connecting with.)

He had done this at several events, but never captured anything to show. That is, until one appearance at a New Age centre in Bolton, Ontario. Benjamin took several pictures that made me light-headed when I looked at them at the end of the night. Others who had stayed afterward to see the photos were equally amazed.

Here is what happened: sometime during the evening, I was drawn to three women in the front of the room who were seated in an L formation — two side by side (daughter and mother), and the third (mother's sister) sitting behind the mother. And when spirit starts directing me, then that is where I have to go.

In my mind's eye, an image was forming. I pointed to a spot that would have been the inside corner of the L, which was a centre point between the three women. "There's someone standing right here," I said, gesturing. "He's right here. And someone else has come in with him."

My husband snapped a picture. And a moment later, another.

I didn't physically "see" the entities, but I had a keen awareness of presence as I described my impressions: two males who looked similar. I felt two brothers — a father and his brother, who would have been an uncle to the daughter in the group. The mother and her sister kept nodding as I spoke, so I knew I was connecting. I then delivered the message from these gentlemen. Unfortunately, I do not remember what I said, but the women listened raptly and seemed glad to hear from them.

After the event, as people were milling around the room while putting on their coats, my husband sought me out and pulled me aside. "You gotta see this!" he said excitedly, then showed me the first photograph (see back cover).

My jaw dropped in surprise. Right where I was pointing — the inside corner of the L, touching the three women — a most glorious circle of white light! And next to the daughter was another orb, larger and fainter than the first. In the next picture, taken a few seconds later, as I continued talking to the women, the orbs were gone. The pictures looked like "before" and "after" shots.

Using the pictures as a guide, we combed the room to see if we could find a logical explanation for the orbs, such as the reflection of the camera flash in the windows (nope; slatted wood blinds covered them), or dust or mist in the air (again, nope; the orbs in photo one were perfectly round, and picture two did not indicate movement, which might have been a sign of dust particles — they vanish).

For months afterward, I was giddy with the knowledge that I, a camera, and spirit had come together at just the right millisecond to record their manifestation. I remember thinking at the time, *I can't wait for it to happen again!* And for the next couple of weeks, we took digital photographs everywhere: out in the backyard, on evening walks around the neighbourhood, while driving over to friends' houses, you name it. But, no orbs in the pictures.

That summer, we packed the camera for a visit to Lily Dale thinking of taking pictures of our friends, but during the trip we began wondering aloud if Lily Dale was the perfect place to go orb hunting. The village has a long history of mediumistic activity, and is rich with stories of spirit contact. Just about every visitor or resident you talk with has a tale of either a haunted house, the sighting of a mysterious presence, or an inexplicable encounter with something that went bump in the night.

Most weekday evenings, the village gets quiet at about 10:00 p.m., after the Sunflower Cafeteria has closed for the night and people who have attended the evening workshops head for the front porch of the Maplewood Hotel to chat with others about the day's events.

As a peaceful hush settled over Lily Dale, Benjamin and I began our walking trip around the grounds. The glittering stars looked like fairy dust against the dark sky. Starting at the front gate, we headed up Cottage Row, clicking pictures as we passed the shuttered auditorium and the nearby octagonal gazebo. Some people sitting on the front porches of their small houses greeted us with friendly hellos and asked us what we were doing; others already knew and were curious if we had photographed anything unusual. Benjamin had captured some interesting objects here and there that we thought might be spirit lights, but nothing seemed to leap off the screen at us. Besides, I wanted to examine the photos later and delete the ones that looked bogus.

At the end of the street, we turned toward Lake Pavilion, which overlooks Cassadaga Lake. Standing inside the porch-like structure and listening to water lapping against the shore, it's simple to understand why the Pavilion is a popular rest spot for Lily Dale visitors. I took a deep, refreshing breath of clean air and enjoyed a moment of serenity. I do not think this little house has changed in seventy years. How many others have stood in this same area and gazed out over the calm waters and the lily pads that resemble floating plates?

Then I sensed a presence with me, and felt as if I were looking at the peaceful world through someone else's eyes. A kind, loving soul who had lived in Lily Dale all his adult life, and enjoyed walking to the Pavilion for a cigarette before going to sleep. In his later years, he walked with a cane, then a walker, and later relied on his next-door neighbour to push him in a wheelchair.

"Please take a picture," I told my husband. As he raised the camera, I added, "one in here, and then one just outside."

The moment the camera's flash exploded light into the Pavilion, I felt the presence vanish. Too bad — I rather liked the chap, and wished I had been able to communicate with him more. Benjamin showed me the camera; the picture revealed nothing of interest. As we walked back onto the ground, I had an idea: what if we asked the spirit people for permission to take their picture?

"Hello," I said to the air, and looked around me. I tried to sound as respectful as possible. "May we please take your picture? We would like to show people who you are. I know how much you loved Lily Dale. We love it, too. Please show yourself to us. We would like to show people proof of spirit."

I nodded to my husband, who raised the camera, aimed it at the night and clicked a picture.

What the camera recorded was an amazing sight. Dozens of white orbs floated in the air, as if someone had released a swarm of phosphorescent balloons. I thought of all the souls who had ever lived here, died here, or even had their ashes scattered over the grounds. (Yes, it is against the law to do that, but …) How many of these spirit people were looking down at us now? I felt surrounded by love.

"They're beautiful," I said and then thanked our invisible visitors.

Benjamin took another picture. The orbs were gone.

For the next five minutes, I could not take my eyes off that wonderful orb-starred photo. We were encircled by orbs — the same way we are surrounded every day by our spirit people: guides, angels, and our loved ones on the other side of the veil. They are with us and, for me, the pictures prove it. Obviously, I cannot say for certain if any of the spirit entities on that photo belonged to me, but even if they did not, it was still comforting to know that the world of spirit was alive and aware of us.

For the next hour or so we walked around taking pictures, and each time we raised the camera, I asked spirit to show themselves. Sometimes they agreed, sometimes they avoided our lens.

"We're like the paparazzi of the paranormal," my husband said.

The front porch of the Maplewood Hotel was filled with late-night talkers. At the far end of the porch, several women were sharing a Nordy's pepperoni pizza that had just been delivered. My husband, ever the mooch, looked hungrily at the triangles of pizza on the ladies' paper plates, but I nudged him into the Maplewood lobby. Out of sight, out of mind; we resumed our spirit-hunting mission.

We tiptoed upstairs to the second floor, hoping to contact the spirit of a Victorian lady who supposedly makes the Maplewood her home. I was not getting an impression of anyone like that, but I was picking up whispers that flitted by like ribbons of breeze. So many people had stayed in this hotel over the last century and had left their imprints in the halls; trying to identify any of these spirits was like trying to separate all the footprints that had been made in a year on a welcome mat.

"Hello," I whispered. "May we please take your picture? Please show yourself to us. We would like to have proof of your spirit, to show people that life continues."

Benjamin shot several pictures down the hall. Then we climbed to the third floor, spoke to spirit, and clicked off a few more. In several photos, you can clearly see orbs in the hallway.

By this time, it was closing in on 11:30 p.m., and I generally start turning into a pumpkin at 10 o'clock. Benjamin wanted to go to the Leolyn Woods and walk to the Stump. I gave him my blessing, then headed to Room 6 and bought a one-way ticket to dreamland.

I saw his pictures the next morning and they were incredible. There are no lights in the woods, so it is like walking in black air. And to make sure you stay on the gravel path, you must shuffle along and listen to your shoes crunching along the trail. If you stop hearing your feet marching through stones, you've entered the woods, where the mosquitoes are licking their lips and telling their friends that dinner has arrived.

> **Our Orb Photos**
> *We had hoped to show you all the orb photographs we mentioned in this chapter but, unfortunately, not all of the photos would reproduce well on the page. And we did not want to do anything to doctor the photos, even if the retouching would make them clearer. So, please go to my website, where I have a special Gallery section entitled "Compassionate Messenger Photos" at* www.carolynmolnar.com/gallery/73.html. *In addition, the gallery also has pictures of Bobby Slash and Lindsay Bolger, whose stories you will read later in this book.*

Benjamin said he spoke to spirit the whole way into the woods, and clicked off two pictures — a "before" and "after" for comparison — every thirty metres or so. And, like I said, some were truly astounding.

In *The Orb Project*, the authors point out that once you develop a persistent interest in photographing orbs, some interesting things begin to happen: these spirit entities start showing up in other photographs. This has begun happening to us in pictures of family gatherings: where, in the corner of the ceiling, is a white ball of light. At my most recent birthday party, hovering over my right shoulder, were three orbs. Furthermore, the authors say, if you allow yourself to see them and celebrate their presence, you will begin to see orbs with your naked eye — in more colour and detail than what is visible to even a digital camera.

I hope I never stop seeing spirit in my photos. And I hope they start appearing in your pictures, too. Who knows? That orb in the upper right hand corner of the picture of your next Christmas family dinner? Maybe it is Grandma stopping by to enjoy the festivities.

Chapter 16

Bobby's Song

You can't judge a soul by its cover. I think about that every time
I remember Bobby Slash, one of my students in a two-day
workshop I taught at Lily Dale in July 2009. Entitled "Back to
Basics: Mediumship 101," the course was designed for everyone
from beginners who wanted to explore their intuitive skills to
experienced mediums who already had a client list. I was hoping
to attract a good mix of skill levels so students would not only
learn from me, but from one another, as well.

I am always a little nervous on the first day of class, so when
I walked into the Assembly Hall and saw three dozen people
facing the podium and looking expectantly at me, I blew off my
jitters with a smile. I whispered a quiet prayer of thanks — there
is nothing worse than offering a class and having no one show

up. In the back of the room, last-minute decision-makers were lined up at the registration desk, hoping to get a seat while others were filling out name tags.

I shuffled my notes at the podium and tried to look authoritative, then glanced at my students and tried to make eye contact with each one. Motion at the back doors caught my eye, and I noticed a large man dressed in black enter the room. His long, straight hair was the colour of midnight. His presence both intimidated and intrigued me. He scribbled something onto a nametag, then walked quietly up the aisle. Energetically, I felt he held secrets and knew more about life than he was willing to let on. When he took a seat, it was to the side of the room, and I wondered why he was keeping himself away from rest of class. His name tag read "Bobby." I pegged him as a "prove it to me" guy, the kind of student who would sit with his arms crossed over his chest and treat everything I said as if I were talking with a mouth full of marbles.

The first day of my workshop was devoted to theory, with a few fun exercises thrown in to break the ice and help the budding mediums gain some confidence. Most of my students were predominantly new to intuitive development, but were eager to learn about their emerging psychic skills. I was also blessed to have several full-time mediums who were in the class to sharpen their abilities and learn a few new techniques.

I led the class through several guided meditations aimed at accessing one's guides and higher self. Before we ended the day, I urged students to continue developing their intuitive sensitivity by joining a meditation circle when they went back to their hometowns; these groups are often advertised in the back section of local New Age newspapers.

One young woman said there were no circles in her very conservative city and asked if there were other ways to practise psychic development. I advised her to try this exercise: get a newspaper and look at the photograph above the story. Without reading the headline or story, study the picture and see if you can pick up any impressions on what the picture is illustrating. Photographs capture the energy of a person or place — what is that energy telling you? Then read the story: how close were you to guessing what that story was about?

Another woman volunteered her method of practice: she closed her eyes, opened the phone book, and put her finger on a name. Then she would see what information she could pick up on that person. I told her that was a good practice, but it was limiting — how could she tell if the information was correct? "After all," I said, "you can't just call a stranger and ask something like, 'Has your sister died recently?'"

Bobby sat quietly that first day, taking notes and occasionally nodding his head at a point I made. After class, I accompanied a couple students to Cup-a-Joe's for some homemade lemonade and a snack, then headed back to my room at the Maplewood Hotel. I always need a nap after teaching. But there was Bobby on the front porch, wearing Roy Orbison-like sunglasses and a Cheshire Cat grin as he rocked back and forth in a chair, looking like punk rock's ambassador to Spiritualism.

As I walked by, he gave me the kind of big-toothed smile that made me want to ask him, "What's so funny?" And I figured he would wryly answer, "What isn't?"

But that wasn't the case at all. "Good class today," he said. "Thanks."

"I'm glad you enjoyed it."

The rocking chair next to him was empty, and he invited me to sit down. As we chatted for the next hour, I found Bobby Slash to be one of the most fascinating and nicest people I had ever met. He was a big man with a big heart, and he knew more history than an encyclopedia. A native New Yorker, Bobby was a musician who had met and talked politics with John Lennon, and performed with dozens of rock 'n' roll icons of the 1980s and 1990s. He was also a student medium, and counted the Amazing Kreskin as one of his teachers.

Lea, a petite woman with a British accent, and another student from my class, came out onto the front porch. Her green eyes crinkled up when she smiled at Bobby and said, "Thank you" before mentioning that she was off to the 1:00 p.m. Stump message service. We watched her go.

"'Thank you'?" I asked, intrigued.

"I met her yesterday in the cafeteria," Bobby said, rocking gently. "It's her first time at Lily Dale, and she was lonely, and a little scared. And she got a reading about her son at a message service that spooked her." Bobby laughed. "She's a soccer mom, and takes her son's sports very seriously. Anyway, I told her not to be upset, because nothing's written in stone. Then I showed her where the Healing Temple was, and she felt better after sitting in there for awhile."

The more Bobby talked, the more I liked him. I had read him so differently when he had first walked into the class. Now, I could see this robust fellow taking little Lea under his wing. He had a graceful way of talking, and I began to realize that he had the ability to sense what made people tick. And, conversely, his gracious and trusting energy drew people to him.

On the second day of class there was a little more theory coupled with an empowering meditation, and then I wagged my finger at my students and acted like a stern taskmaster — which was hard to do, because Bobby was grinning at me and I had to keep myself from laughing.

"Today," I said, "you guys are gonna work!"

"All right!" a couple of them answered.

I broke the class into two circles of about fifteen students each, and asked everyone in their circle to first give a person-directed message. In other words, the student looked at someone in the circle, asked, "May I come to you?" (you *always* ask permission), and then had to say the first thing that came into his or her head. As expected, there were some hits, some misses, and a lot of giggling. But that was okay, because good mediumship depends on being totally open to spirit and totally free from ego to repeat what spirit whispers into your ear (or places pictures in your head, if you are clairvoyant).

Next, I asked the students to give a spirit-inspired message. A spirit-inspired message is, basically, information spirit gives you, and you often have to figure out who the message is for. So, instead of saying, "May I come to you?" you are asking, "Who can recognize this?"

I bounced back and forth from one circle to the next, listening to my students deliver their messages. Some spoke confidently, while others scrunched their eyes closed, focused in silence, and struggled to speak. To those students, I gave encouraging comments, and tried to make the experience as non-threatening as possible.

Then I turned to Bobby's circle and found it was his turn. I will let him tell his story, which he kindly forwarded to me later in an email:

> What I received from spirit for a woman I was reading for, was a man's name and his birth date. The woman said that made sense, except the person I had mentioned was alive and well. As I turned to look at the person in the circle who was next to speak, you [Carolyn] asked if I could get anything more, because you were

intrigued by the sitter's reply. I concentrated hard, and after about twenty seconds, spirit told me that the children are okay and well, and that the man was at peace. He was at total peace. This confused the woman even more. However, she said she and the man had had several children while they were married.

You then told us that this could happen — the spirit of a very forceful person with a lot of energy could come through while he/she was still on the earth plane. But it didn't happen very often.

Later, as I was sitting on the "good ol' porch" at the Maplewood Hotel, someone came to me and said that I'd done a reading in your class for her friend, and then gave me some very sad news. It turns out that the energy of the man that I'd picked up had died about one hour before I gave the message. Well … it just blew me away. The thought of delivering such a powerful and meaningful message at such a crucial time.… As you say: "The power and wisdom of spirit!!" I burst out into tears. I know that some of those tears were happy, shocked tears over what I had accomplished, BUT they were mostly tears about how the woman and her children were, knowing that her ex-husband had just died.

After that, I did some meditation asking my spirit guides questions, BUT also thanking them and spirit for coming to me (as I always do).

Having studied the art of mentalism and becoming friends with the Amazing Kreskin has taught me a lot about preparing to become a medium. It was funny how, when I first saw you giving messages at the Forest Temple, another medium told me: "You don't need books or classes to be a medium. Just do it!!" Which is all fine and well, BUT it never ever hurts to continue to learn in life. And I have to say that YOUR class was such a great learning experience. I strongly recommend it!!

I felt that I learned soooo much, that I'm planning to put up a picture frame with our class picture, your book and CD on my wall in the future. So when people ask, "Who is that?" I can reply, "One of my BEST Teachers." I have a song entitled "Peace Within the Light" and I will write it about you (with your permission, of course).

When Bobby signed off his email with that last paragraph — well, how could I not want to give him a big congratulatory hug?

Permission granted, of course. (I am flattered.)

What made Bobby's feat so amazing was that he was able to contact someone who had passed *just one hour* before he delivered his message. And, what is more, the experience is also a testament to the fellow who passed; though he was divorced from his wife, he cared about her and their children so much that he did whatever he could to get through to her and tell her he was all right.

Bobby — I hope you continue to develop your mediumistic skills. And I am looking forward to hearing your song on my next birthday.

• • •

I wrote the above story and posted it in September 2009 as a blog on my website. A few days later, I placed a sticky note on my computer with this reminder: "Call Bobby on my birthday." I wanted him to sing me his song.

Sadly, I never got to hear him sing. In February 2010, I received this email from Scott Gordon, one of Bobby's friends:

"Bobby has passed through his transition to the next life at approximately 2 a.m. He was in the hospital for pneumonia, from which he never recovered. I didn't know if anyone else had thought to inform you of this, but he thought very highly of you and I thought I should pass on the information."

I read the note, then reread it again, unable to consider the words in front of me. My mouth hung open in disbelief. I felt like I had swallowed a cold stone. Bobby was such a strong, strapping man, and so full of life! *Is this true, Bobby?* I asked with my mind, sending that thought into the universe. But I did not feel his presence. *Talk to me, Bobby,* I urged. *Let me know you're okay.* If anyone would understand the importance of spirit communication, it would be the two of us.

I felt nothing, and wondered if the email had been a cruel joke. But why would someone do that to me? I wrote back to the person who had first sent me the notice, and anxiously waited for his answer back.

Two days later I received this, from his life partner, Ana:

I am emailing you the sad news that my honey, Bobby Slash, passed away this past Wednesday, February 3, 2010. He was fighting a bad cold that turned into pneumonia, which hit him very hard and ended up triggering all kinds of complications in his body. I am still trying to get over the loss of my love. We were talking about getting married soon and have been living together for now five years now.

He has passed, but is in a better place and at peace. I can see that he enjoyed your company at the Lily Dale workshop and it will never be forgotten. I know he will work on his spiritual gifts on the other side, so don't be shocked if you hear from him.

I was looking forward to going again to Lily Dale with Bobby and hopefully meet you one day. We went there this August and it was beautiful, with the leaves so colourful and we had the best quiet time and couple time ever. He mentioned he was going to write a song for you; I found it and have noted it below. It is a gift Bobby would have wanted you to have. I am going to see if I can compose music for the words on my own with my guitar and when I do, I will send it to you.

God Bless … Ana

Scott later contacted me again to say Bobby's memorial service was "crowded to overflowing."

I can believe it. I wish I had been there.

Bobby's passing was — and continues to be — a huge loss. All of his talent and physical life force: gone. I was so looking forward to seeing him at Lily Dale again, rocking beside me on the Maplewood's front porch and listening to him spin more tales of the New York City street scene.

As a medium, I can be in touch with his presence, but it is not the same as actually seeing a knowing grin. When I work with spirit, it is communication at arm's length. I am not face to face with someone. Don't get me wrong, I love talking with spirit — but it can sometimes be a poor substitute for listening to someone you enjoy tell a joke, sharing a basket of sweet potato fries, or receiving a loving hug.

I try to look for lessons in all my experiences, and when I think about Bobby, I realize that we never fully appreciate how delicate our physical body can be, and how much stronger the spirit body is, so when the physical body cannot handle a trauma, we go back to spirit. You just never know when the physical self will give out, and you can never really prepare yourself for the last time you will see somebody. Therefore, it is so important to value every moment.

I miss Bobby, and I know his spirit will come to me when he is ready. At this point, with his passing so fresh, I think he is with his own people — the ones he grew up with, the ones hurting more than I. And I know his generous and sensitive soul has found peace within the light.

With many thanks to Ana Serrano, here are Bobby's lyrics:

Peace Within the Light
Words that are well spoken
Lessons to be learned
Students in her workshop
Gifts to be earned
A teacher of much knowledge
And very down to earth
Spirit guides amongst us
An awakening — just like birth

An inspiration to us all
Move ahead — do not fall

Bobby's Song

Listen to (learn from) spirit's call
Peace within the light

There is an age-old saying
That everything happens for reason
To have her as a friend of mine
Is a blessing for all seasons
Truly an inspiration
That's what she is to me
So I will write this song for her
So everyone can see

An inspiration to us all
Move ahead — do not fall
Listen to (learn from) spirit's call
Peace within the light

— Bobby Slash

Chapter 17

Lost Spirits

My friends Helen and Phil Heinz had begun to wonder if something else besides their family was inhabiting their beautiful three-storey Tudor-style house in tony Etobicoke. Three weeks after the couple and their young daughters, Amelia and Jane, had moved into the home, the Heinzs began to suspect their dream house contained the stuff that nightmares are made of.

Built in the early 1900s for a wealthy retailer, the house still had its original hardwood floors, bright cherry-wood ceiling beams, and huge leaded windows that overlooked a tree-lined street. Each room was spacious, from the cluster of bedrooms on the top floor to the basement area, which the previous owners had sectioned into an exercise area, a den, and an unfinished laundry room. At one time, the basement had contained servants' quarters.

On most mornings, the sunlight slanting into the kitchen bathed the room in a cheery glow. Phil, an investment analyst, liked taking his coffee there before heading to work. Sometimes he dawdled on the way to his office, just so he could linger awhile at the kitchen table with eight-year-old Amelia and five-year-old Jane.

But the house seemed to change when Phil and the kids were gone. Certain areas of the house made Helen uncomfortable — especially the laundry room located beneath the stairs. At times, there seemed to be a heaviness in the little alcove, and walking into the closet-sized room made her feel sad. At times, she glanced down at the floor, expecting to see someone looking up at her. And then one night, as she was leaving the room with an armload of towels, she thought she saw a small shadow scoot by her legs.

She dismissed that apparition, certain that the creepy room was making her mind play tricks on her. But a few nights later she saw a similar dark shape flit through the bedroom and vanish into the side wall. The couple's bedroom, she realized, was located exactly two floors above the laundry room.

The shadow appeared intermittently over the next several weeks. Sometimes, if she turned her head quickly, she saw the dark blur in the corner of her eye. But when she tried to look at that shadow straight on, she saw nothing.

"Phil," she said, nudging her husband in bed one evening, "did you see that?"

"Hmmmm?" he answered, gazing up from the business section of the *Globe and Mail*.

As the days went by, and the shape began showing itself more frequently in the basement and her bedroom, Helen began wondering if there a presence in the house. What if it was evil? Could her family be in danger? And what was it about the laundry room that evoked in her such deep feelings of regret?

Then again, she reasoned, *I'm the only one experiencing these things. Maybe it's my active imagination.*

But that changed one morning when Jane, her youngest, asked at breakfast, "Mommy, why was Daddy crying last night?"

"Daddy wasn't crying," Helen said cautiously. "Why do you say that?"

Jane continued eating her crunchy breakfast cereal. "I heard him. He was crying."

Helen turned to Amelia and asked in a voice that did not betray her concern, "Did you hear something, too?"

Amelia looked at her sister and shrugged.

"Honey?" Helen prompted.

"I'm mad at her," Amelia said. "She takes my toys and never puts them back in the right places!"

"I do not!"

Helen quieted her children and sent them off to school. Later that morning, worried for the safety of her family, she called me for help.

I told Helen that I am not a ghostbuster. I had not done a house clearing since my very first client more than twenty years ago. I do not choose to do soul rescue work with lost spirits, because I prefer working with clients who bring spirit that *want* to be with me. Hauntings involve different types of energies: they may be confused or angry, or unwilling to be released. And some spirit, despite any kind of soul rescue work, will not budge from the house. They feel the space is theirs, and *you* are the trespasser.

Helen asked, "Well, can you just tell me if you're picking anything up? Is it evil?"

I concentrated for a moment and tuned into Helen's vibrational energy. "I'm not getting the sense that you're in danger. But have you had a guest recently who was very depressed?"

"Now I've got goosebumps," Helen said, and proceeded to lure me over with the promise of homemade spinach lasagna for lunch. Plus homemade blueberry pie for dessert. Served heated, with a scoop of Avondale French vanilla ice cream on the side. Oh, well … what are friends for?

• • •

As the tantalizing scent of lasagna began to waft from the oven, Phil played upstairs with the couple's daughters while Helen and I tiptoed down to the basement.

Two stationary bicycles stood side by side in the exercise area; one was still wrapped in plastic. "I don't like being down here," Helen whispered. I walked between the bikes and around the barbell rack, and did not feel anything. Ditto in the den, though I admired the fireplace and big-screen TV.

We entered the laundry room, which was still a work in progress. The air smelled musty, like boxes of old books in the back of a closet. Dim light from a bulb dangling from the ceiling made the room seem forlorn. There were hairline cracks in the plaster, and a small hole at the bottom of a wall looked like it had once been a bigger gap that had been hastily repaired. I began to believe that Helen's feelings of distress were due to the dingy atmosphere of this unfinished room, and she would be happier once the walls were scraped and painted a brighter colour —

Suddenly, something squeezed my heart. An immense sadness filled my chest, and I wanted to flee. My heart beat fast and tears stung my eyes.

I hurried out of the room. Once in the hall, I gulped cold air and waited for the mild dizziness to pass.

"Are you all right?" asked Helen, who was now at my side.

I nodded. In my mind's eye, I had seen the face of a terrified little boy — maybe six or seven years old. His coffee-coloured hair was mussed and there were smudges of dirt on his cheeks. He wore a torn shirt and leggings from the 1920s. But the place was not a laundry room in the 1920s; it had been a storage space, and the hole in the wall then was just big enough for a small child to squeeze into....

Oh, God, I prayed, *please do not tell me there is a child's body in the hole.*

My guides quickly calmed me, whispering gently to me that this wasn't so. Relieved, I let my heartbeat settle, then turned to Helen and told her what I'd just envisioned.

"Yes," Helen said, confirming my hunch. "I've often felt the presence of a young boy down here."

I went inward, concentrating on the spirit of the boy to bring him closer. I felt the child's loneliness. He was also hungry, tired, and frightened.

And very sad. But what could I do to help him?

Helen and I stepped back into the laundry room. I concentrated again, asked the spirit to show himself ... then felt the energy of the scared spirit approach.

"What is your name, please, and why are you here?" I asked softly.

I can't let them find me, I heard. *Mommy will get in trouble. Where is she?*

In my mind, I asked the boy to tell me about himself. I saw a picture of a maid, and realized she was the boy's mother. She had been a servant at the house, and was not allowed to bring her children to work with her. One day, the boy was too ill to be left alone in her apartment, so she smuggled him into the house and hid him in the crawlspace. She visited him for a few minutes whenever she could sneak away from her duties, but her check-ins were infrequent because she was afraid of getting fired. At first the boy enjoyed this hide-and-seek game, but the basement was cold and damp, and ... it was so cold in the house....

"What is your name?" I asked him.

Tommy, he responded hesitantly. *But don't tell anyone. I promised Mommy no one would find me.*

I asked Tommy why he was still in the house, and he said he was waiting for his mother. I tried to find out how he had passed, but the boy refused to believe that he had died!

It's so cold here. Where's my Mommy?

"I want to help you," I said. "I'm going to show you where it's warm. And, I am going to try to find your mommy." In my mind, I imagined a brilliant, white light, the beautiful shimmering luminescence that is the portal between the physical plane and the world of spirit.

"Do you see the light?" I asked Tommy.

Yes.

"Does it feel warm?"

Yes. I like it.

"Do you see your mommy in the light?"

Yes.

"Would you like to go into the light to get a hug from her?"

I can't. I felt him pull away from me. He was crying. *I can't find my shoe! Mommy will be mad!*

"No, she won't," I said comfortingly, then asked my guides to bring the boy's mother closer to Tommy and me. Thankfully, it only took a moment and then a doe-eyed woman whose face shined with love felt the vibration. Her name was Ruth, I was told. Ruth had passed into the light not long after her child had died of scarlet fever; her heart had just given out. Perhaps she had died of a broken heart, because losing her child had saddened her. In fact, Ruth in spirit had been looking for her child, too.

In my mind's eye, I saw Ruth embrace her son, take his hand, and, minus one shoe, walk with him into the light.

Instantly, I felt a change of pressure in the room.

Even Helen felt the change. "I don't feel sad anymore," she said. "I think he's gone."

Indeed, the Heinz family no longer senses the sad presence in their home. It was also a relief for Helen to feel that Tommy had been reunited with his mom. Whether we are moms in the physical or in spirit, we understand what it feels like to have a child who is lost. A family reunion, even from beyond the grave, is such a sweet experience.

And, by the way, the lasagna was delicious.

• • •

Tommy was a lost spirit. I prefer the word "lost" over "trapped," which some mediums and psychics prefer, because "trapped" for me implies something that is ensnared, caught like a mouse in a cage. I believe it is natural for our soul to want to return to the source after our time on Earth is done — but, sometimes, at the moment of transition, the mind confuses the soul and it gets lost. The mind remembers the fear or guilt it experienced when it lived in the body, and after the body passes, the mind becomes afraid of a punishing God or ashamed of its earthly actions and becomes too guilty to pass into the light.

Case in point: Frederika, a very agitated and worried York University student who telephoned one day, begging for a medium to come to her dorm room. For the past month, just before going to bed at night, she had heard a man with a low voice talking to her. At first, she thought it was someone's boyfriend in the next room, but the women living on both sides of her told her they were not the kind of girls that had — *ahem* — gentleman callers.

"He talks to you?" I asked. "What does he say?"

"I can't make out the words," she answered. "But I know he's there. I asked my guides for help, but he won't go away."

Frederika, a gregarious second-year student majoring in history, lived in one of the older dorms on campus. Old dorms, like old apartment buildings, have seen a lot of residents — which means there is a pretty good chance that over the years, a lost soul could have attached itself to someone in the living. And when that resident moved on, the entity stayed.

I made an appointment to visit Frederika's dorm, then called my friend Stella, who has cleaned more houses than a Hoover. I told her very little about Frederika, but Stella said she felt a tingle in her spine when I mentioned the words "dorm room" — a good indication that there was, indeed, a spirit that needed some help to cross over.

We visited Frederika on a frosty November afternoon, where the cold rain was just a few degrees away from snowflakes. Frederika's one-room shoebox apartment had all the trappings of a college student: shelves of books, a wooden table bought at a Value Village that also served as a desk, a foldout bed, and two mismatched end tables covered with neat stacks of papers. Her most prized possession was an electric tea kettle.

The moment I entered the room, I felt a whispered chill. Yes, there was something — or someone — with us. Stella and I exchanged looks as I sat next to Frederika on her bed; Stella took the desk chair.

"There's a male presence here," Stella said.

The room suddenly grew colder. I sensed a middle-aged man with a bit of a paunch. As I thought about him, I felt his energy get bigger. And then he sat "in" me; his coldness permeated me.

But I did not feel his spirit was trying to possess me. He wanted attention, I felt him say. He was not related to Frederika, and had no connection to the university. He was lost between two worlds, ignored by both. And he was looking for a way to be heard.

What is your name? I asked him in my mind, but he would not answer.

I persisted. *Why are you here?*

I felt a hesitancy, then, *I have nowhere else to go.*

What about your family? I asked.

I'm alone. I can't go back to Scotland.

Why not? I waited for an answer; either he did not know or was refusing to tell me. I repeated my earlier question: *Why are you here?*

I'm attracted to her lights.

That is when Stella and I noticed all the crystals in the room. Then we looked at Frederika, and we saw her lit up like a Christmas tree. Her chakras — her body's energy centres — were very open. Frederika's problem was she did not know how to close them; she was doing the right things by working with her guides and angels, but her soul light burned so brightly that she attracted wandering entities like a magnet picking up iron filings.

But first things first. "Let's help this entity pass over," I said, and the three of us held hands. Stella said a prayer asking for divine help, and we followed that with a few minutes of silence, where we each asked our guides to help this entity home, so he could cross over into the light. We meditated on that for a few more minutes ... and then we felt the room become less congested. The air grew lighter, warmer.

Frederika smiled.

The spirit had transitioned. We said another silent prayer to thank our otherworldly helpers, then closed our soul rescue circle.

Before we left, we told Frederika how to close herself down and protect herself from hitchhiking entities that might be attracted to the light of her beautiful soul. We asked her to meditate daily and concentrate on the health of her energy centres. Imagine your chakras as wheels that are the size of side plates, I said. This size is "normal" and will not attract spirit to you, for you will no longer be a beacon to them.

Often, lost spirits give out a cry for help. Something was missed during their transition from life to the afterlife, and they are looking for answers to help them understand their situation. Ghosts are not to be feared. Mostly, they just need help.

Chapter 18

Our Children's Voices

I was a little nervous about the upcoming session. It was a crisp January evening, and I stood at the window in my office that overlooks the street, waiting for six ladies from Georgetown who were making a special trip to see me. The women were members of a bereavement group, and all had lost a child within the last year. I believe that doing work for hospice and bereavement groups is the highest form of service I can perform. Yet these sessions are often hard for me because, as a mother who has experienced all the bumps and bruises and scares that come with raising two children, I can only imagine the terrible heartbreak of losing a child.

Please, spirit, I prayed in thought, as I gazed up into the clear night sky, *let me help these women.*

A few minutes later, two Honda SUVs pulled up to the curb before my office and six bundled ladies stepped out of the vehicles. Their breath made plumes of smoke in the frosty air. Several looked like they were sharing a joke. I noticed how brightly coloured many of their coats were. *Silly me*, I thought, expecting these women to arrive in silence and dressed in black.

I met them at the front door, then ushered them into the reception area. We made pleasant conversation about this and that; several had seen the latest Sandra Bullock movie and highly recommended it. Then we talked about the arctic air that was due to blow in this weekend (we Canadians love to talk about the weather!) and one lady, an avid gardener, gave me a few tips on how to protect my temperamental rose bushes, which are probably hoping to be reincarnated as cacti in Arizona in their next lifetime.

As we chatted, I noticed that the woman who had introduced herself as Bonnie seemed to stay in the background. She was a tall, striking brunette dressed simply in a white blouse and dark slacks. For some reason, I wanted to reach out to her and draw her into the conversation. From the corner of my eye, I saw her watching me, but whenever I looked at her, her gaze was elsewhere.

As our chatting wound down, I gestured to my reading room and asked, "Who would like to go first?"

The ladies exchanged tentative glances. Lisbet, the leader of the group, said, "Well, we talked about it, and wondered if you could speak to us all together."

I told them that was not how I usually worked; I focus better in one-on-one sessions. That way, a client can give me a picture of the loved one in spirit that she would like me to try to connect with, or an object that once belonged to the individual, and I can put my full attention only on that spirit.

"We all brought pictures," Lisbet said eagerly, as she pulled a photograph from a purse emblazoned with John Lennon's face. "Besides, we all know each other so well, and we like to think our children have gotten to know each other, too."

The ladies rearranged the wingback chairs and couches in my reception area to form a circle, then passed me their pictures. Four boys and two girls. Each with a lovely smile and shining eyes filled with hope. I gazed at each one, then put them on the table in the middle of the circle and closed my eyes to centre myself. I did not know how old these children were when they had passed, nor did I know how recent the pictures were, yet none of them looked younger than teenagers. I asked my guides for help, then began speaking.

The first voice I heard had me blushing. "Oh, dear," I said. "He's talking about beer and being at the cottage. He swears a lot, but in a fun way. He liked to be the life of the party. He's telling me he was six-foot-two in his boots, and he's hoping you're taking good care of his motorcycle."

A woman named Agnes laughed loudly. "That sounds like my Franklin."

"No, Frank," I said. "He's telling me he hated Franklin. He kept correcting you whenever you called him Franklin. And there's something about a panda bear."

Agnes was chuckling, yet she had tears in her eyes as she pulled a key chain from her pants pocket. A panda bear figurine dangled from it. "Franklin's — excuse me, Frank's — nickname was 'Panda.' When we brought him home from the hospital, he had such big eyes, my husband said he looked like a panda bear. And the name stuck."

We shared a laugh, and so it went for several hours. The mothers received evidence that, yes, their children were visiting them from spirit and, yes, they still loved and watched over their families. They all appreciated being remembered at their birthdays and the anniversaries of their passing. Some spirit came in gently, being just as shy or quiet as they were in life. And through it all, Frank acted like the party host, boisterously encouraging his spirit friends to connect with their parents. And the mothers laughed and cried, happy to know that their children were happy, yet sad because they all missed their kids.

Except for Bonnie. While she laughed along with her companions as they experienced joy, I had not been able to bring her child across. I wondered if Bonnie's daughter was angry with her? (Unfortunately, it happens sometimes — for some reason, the spirit does not want to connect with the client.) *Please, guys, I begged my guides, give me something for Bonnie!*

I looked at her. Our eyes locked.

Suddenly, I said, "It's not your fault."

Bonnie turned away and hid her face as she burst into tears. Quickly, her friends surrounded her, comforting her with hugs and gentle words. Giving Bonnie that simple sentence seemed to loosen whatever was blocking the moment, and her daughter came through to tell me of the hurt she now realized she had brought to her family, and how sorry she was that things had turned out the way they did.

"I know you tried," I said, hearing the teenager's choked voice in my head. "I made some bad choices. But please know that I love you."

The room was quiet for several minutes. Even Bonnie's tears fell silently. Exhausted, I sank into a chair and sent loving thoughts to the women supporting their hurting friend.

Eventually, the energy in the room began to shift as I felt the spirits of these ladies' children depart. Bonnie's daughter was the last to go, but not before she gave her mother a hug. In my mind, I saw her whisper something into Bonnie's ear. At that moment, Bonnie drew in a deep breath and lowered her head. She touched her cheek, then raised her head and smiled.

No one spoke, even though I sensed everyone had a lot to say. So I stood and asked, "Is it time for tea?" Yes, the women agreed, and began talking among themselves as I left the room to start the peppermint tea brewing.

At the end of the evening, I thanked the ladies for coming and walked them back to their cars. The air was so cold, I felt like I could peel it off my face. The cars sputtered to life and these grieving yet brave mothers began their long drive home. Before I went back into my office, I looked up into the sky. The stars seemed to be twinkling a little brighter. Then I called my son and daughter at university, and listened to their voices.

○ ○
○ ○

Chapter 19

Lindsay's Story

○ ○
○ ○

This is Lindsay's story. But it is also Jo-Ann's story to tell, and John belongs to this story, too. My sister even owns a piece of this story. In fact, this story belongs to everyone who believes in the power of hope, and understands that we all have the gift to touch thousands of lives.

• • •

September 2005

My sister and I were having lunch at one of our favourite restaurants, a quaint little homestyle eatery in Unionville, when she mentioned a medical crisis that friends of her family were undergoing. John and Jo-Ann Bolger's daughter, Lindsay, had surgery to remove a brain tumour in April 2005. Jo-Ann had told my sister the previous day that the tumour was showing signs of regrowth. More surgery was being discussed and doctors were advising Lindsay against enrolling for her final year in university.

As my sister was telling me Lindsay's story, I closed my eyes and unconsciously began tuning into Lindsay's energy. "It's behind her right ear," I said, then caught my breath as a heaviness settled on my spine and thoughts of sadness washed through me. I did not want to cry.

I described the shape of the tumour and advised my sister to tell the Bolgers to seek out more support with a naturopath. But in the pit of my stomach, I knew Lindsay was gravely ill. I felt concentric circles of strong love and support surrounding her; Lindsay's family and many friends were doing their best to protect and support her physically, emotionally, and spiritually. Yet I felt in the future that the Bolgers would experience profound sorrow, and their grief was like a great grey cloud floating over their house.

I did not want to cry.

I begged my guides to give me something hopeful to give Lindsay and her family. "Despite these troubles, she will graduate university," I said, and felt relieved.

Then I cried.

My sister sat quietly during this. My tears surprised her, because I have always been known as the family stoic. She does not put a lot of stock in what I do for a living, but at least she does not hang her head in shame whenever I walk into the room, so she is okay in my book. Healthy skepticism beats total dismissal any day.

That evening, she telephoned the Bolgers at their house in Markham, and inquired about Lindsay's health. My sister fumbled with her words for a few moments before saying, "I don't know how to tell you this, but my sister sees things."

"Huh?" Jo-Ann said. The Bolgers are a very pragmatic couple; she is a teacher and John sells software.

"Well," my sister said, "Carolyn's sort of a psychic. You can do what you want with this, but let me tell you what she told me this afternoon," she said, and proceeded to repeat our lunch conversation.

Jo-Ann surprised my sister by saying, "Is there any way we could meet her?"

● ● ●

April 2005 — Jo-Ann's Story

Lindsay telephoned us from Antigonish, Nova Scotia, complaining of excruciating headache pain. Just shy of her twenty-second birthday, Lindsay was a bright, athletic young woman pursuing a kinesiology degree at St. Francis Xavier University. Her goal was to work in sports medicine. Blond and hazel-eyed, she worked out every day, played rugby and volleyball at university, and taught swimming in the summer, so she knew how to play through bumps, bruises, and muscle strains. But her head pain had been so intolerable, she had gone to the emergency room three times in five days.

Once, a doctor who thought her headaches were stress-related, advised her to get a massage. John contacted the emergency room and insisted if Lindsay showed up there again, they must do a CT scan. Determined that Lindsay's case wouldn't fall through the cracks, I followed up by calling the hospital for the test results.

After being put on hold several times, a doctor got on the phone. "It's a good thing you asked us to order a scan," he said solemnly. "Unfortunately, your daughter has a brain tumour."

I think at that moment, the world stopped spinning. I swallowed hard and listened in shock as the doctor described the peach-pit-sized mass on the outside of her brain, just behind the right ear. As I cradled the phone, I felt dizzy and then paralyzed, as if I were looking through the doorway to a room that I was terrified to enter.

John and I dropped everything and flew to Nova Scotia. We met Lindsay in a hospital in Halifax, where her friends had driven her. Further CT scans showed the tumour had penetrated her brain and physicians advised surgery. "I wouldn't delay an operation," one doctor said, "but I wouldn't be offended if you wanted to take her home." We arranged for the surgery to be performed at Toronto Western Hospital.

The procedure went well and Lindsay was upbeat. When the surgeon visited her hospital room, she looked him in the eye and said, "Give me the straight facts. If it's good, it's good. If it's bad, I'll deal with it." That was the kind of girl she was. She never liked sugar-coating a situation. She felt that if she was honest with the world, then the world had an obligation to be honest with her.

The doctor felt the operation had removed most of the tumour, but radiation treatments were necessary because surgery hadn't gotten all of it. He described what those treatments would be like, and that Lindsay would lose some of her beautiful blonde hair. She quietly digested his words, nodding a few times as she resigned herself to the process.

That evening, I sat beside Lindsay as she lay in bed watching TV. The hospital was quiet that night, but I didn't hear the silence. I just watched my daughter and thought about all the times I had sat up with her when she was sick with measles, or mumps, or a bad cough. I watched her chest move up and down in slow, even breaths. I wished I could take whatever was making her feel ill and put it in a jar and bury it in the ground. I was scared, and I could sense she was scared. Then, as if she was reading my mind, she took my hand, and gave it a reassuring squeeze. Lindsay's eyes were on the television, and I followed her line of sight. She was watching *The Amazing Race.* "This is going to be like our amazing race," she said.

At Princess Margaret Hospital in Toronto, Lindsay underwent stereotactic radiation therapy five days a week for six weeks. Under this non-surgical procedure, a high-dose beam of precisely-targeted radiation is directed at a specific area of the brain. A section of her head was shaved to prepare for the treatment, and Lindsay wondered how much more of her silky hair she would lose.

At the hospital, we saw heavily sedated children, ranging in age from two to five years old, with totally shaved heads, preparing for their radiation treatments. Watching these youngsters so cruelly afflicted, I saw tears forming in Lindsay's eyes. "My God," she said once, her voice a whisper, "I'm never going to complain again."

We were talking about her hair loss and she thought about wearing a baseball cap to hide the shaving marks on her scalp, when she had the idea of doing something that would help others who might be facing the same issues she was. A baseball cap that was also a symbol of empowerment, and the logo on the cap would be a "B" (for Bolger) that was made with a loop similar to the "Remember Our Troops" ribbons. The "B" would also stand for "B-Strong", which played off Lance Armstrong's motto: "Livestrong." She had read Armstrong's book and was inspired by his journey to overcome cancer. We found a place that made caps and ordered one hundred for her friends and family, to show support for her. If she wore the cap, we would too. Well, not only did her friends want the caps, but friends of those friends wanted to buy the cap, and all her teammates at university. We ended up ordering 350 caps and sold them all. The caps became a fundraiser for brain cancer research.

The next two months were recovery time for Lindsay as she got her strength back. We enjoyed spending lots of summer time together, and I looked forward to having my family healed again. But in August, a CT scan found that the tumour had started to grow again. In pictures, it was a smooth-edged opaque mass with smaller high-density masses within it. Lindsay's oncologist suggested taking a year off to rest.

"No," Lindsay argued. "You've taken away my energy, you've taken away my hair, and you're not taking away my graduating year."

It was so hard taking her back to Nova Scotia that fall. But imagine our surprise when we pulled up to St. Francis Xavier and saw all the varsity athletes wearing B-Strong caps in support of Lindsay. Everyone knew what she was struggling through. She was so moved. I forced myself to not cry in front of her.

Going home, I sat in an airport restaurant and burst into tears. Then, when I was back home, unpacking my luggage, I found a note in my suitcase, reading: *I'll be fine. Don't worry about me. I'm just a phone call away.*

I wished I knew the future. I wanted so badly for Lindsay's story to have a happy ending. I thought about that phone call from Antigonish, and the doctor who'd told me in his clinical voice, "It's a good thing you asked us to order a scan." On that day, the world had changed and there was nothing I could do to get everything back on the right track. And that didn't seem fair.

I drifted through the next couple days and sent my daughter a prayer as often as I could.

When Carolyn's sister called, my antennas went up. I'm pretty skeptical about this psychic stuff. But I was intrigued by what Carolyn said, and asked if I could meet her.

Both sisters came over. I thought Carolyn would look like a gypsy, with a large skirt, peasant top, big earrings, and large puffy hair. But she wore slacks and a jacket, and looked like a normal, ordinary person. I made tea, and John and I gathered around the island in the kitchen to listen to what she had to say. I expected her to make a bunch of predictions, but that didn't happen.

She told us, among other things, that Lindsay would achieve a "celebrity status," she would seek out a naturopath in Antigonish, and there would be a connection to a medical doctor east of Toronto who would help her. Lindsay would also need more surgery and radiation, and she would be on medication for the rest of her life. But she also said Lindsay would always remain positive through this ordeal, and her story would be known. Carolyn then advised us about doctors she was familiar with.

The next day, Atlantic TV called Lindsay at her school. They wanted to do a story on her B-Strong caps, and how she was turning her courageous struggle with cancer into a cause that was helping others. CTV's *Canada AM* called her a few days later, also wanting to do a story. After those reports aired, we sold one thousand hats across Canada, and raised thousands of dollars for brain tumour research. We also began getting letters from people thanking us, reaching out to us for support, and saying things like, "My mother was just diagnosed with brain cancer" or "My father has been diagnosed with prostate cancer."

And I thought, "Oh my God. 'Celebrity status.'"

• • •

September 2005 — John's Story

Lindsay began seeing a naturopath in Antigonish as she continued working toward her kinesiology degree. She was also active in athletics during her senior year, though to a different degree — she helped manage the rugby team, which went to Victoria, British Columbia, for national finals.

She took medication to control her headaches and mini-blackouts, but in January 2006, she had a grand mal seizure. Unfortunately, the seizure meant she had to surrender her driver's license, which devastated her. Physicians urged her to leave school, but graduating was so important to her. She was not the kind of person to leave anything undone.

The Maritimes is beautiful in late spring, and the St. Francis Xavier campus was lush with greenery for the May graduation. Flowers scented the air. The arts faculty named Lindsay valedictorian, and we attended a special lunch with the university president, the kinesiology program director, the athletics director, and the coach of the rugby team.

Watching her march down the aisle in her graduation robe — royal blue gown with gold lapel — was such a proud moment for us, because we knew this had not come easy for her. We sat in the front row and cried tears of joy. And when she mounted the stage for her diploma, we couldn't wipe the smiles off our faces. I held my wife's hand and my heart felt like all the problems in the world were in someone else's life a million miles away.

When she got up to deliver the valedictory speech, the hall was silent. She didn't talk about herself, but referred to friends of hers, and referred to people who, no matter what kinds of challenges they faced, marched on toward success. Life is so precious, I thought at that moment, and every heartbeat is so important. It's what makes us human. She finished to thunderous applause and a standing ovation. I wiped my eyes, and then Jo-Ann, her grandma, and I ran up to her with bouquets of flowers.

That summer, an MRI found the tumour growing again. Doctors decided to start her on chemotherapy, because radiation couldn't be done again in the same area. Along with the chemo, the doctors advised rest, but Lindsay would have none of that. She wanted to get on with her life, and enrolled at George Brown College to pursue a sports marketing management degree. That was just like her: every time something came along to knock her down, she just picked herself up and continued planning her life as if nothing was going wrong. She was even looked at wedding dresses, though she wasn't dating anyone, and thought of which songs she wanted at her reception.

One of her class assignments was a group activity to create a charity fundraiser. She took charge of her group and devised a project to benefit brain tumour research. Playing off her caps, she organized "The B-Strong Bash" and found sponsors, caterers, and people to donate items for a silent auction. I figured if we sold two hundred to three hundred tickets at $50 each, we'd cover our costs. Well, we got five hundred people and raised $65,000 that was split between four hospitals: The Princess Margaret Hospital Foundation (Toronto), Montreal Neurological Institute and Hospital, Sick Kids Foundation (Toronto), and Sunnybrook Foundation (Toronto).

The Bash was held on November 16, 2007 — Jo-Ann's birthday. And the best part about the event? The look of surprise on Lindsay's face when she saw how many friends and neighbours came out to support her cause. My band, UnderCover, played that night, mostly 1960s and 1970s pop. We also played the theme to *Friends*, one of her favourite songs.

Lindsay's group received an A+ on the project.

2008 wasn't a good year. In spring, Lindsay had her fourth surgery, and while doctors were able to remove some cysts, the procedure left her without vision in the left side of both eyes. She had trouble sleeping, and outside of school, didn't want to socialize.

That summer she told me, "Okay, we're planning the next Bash." Later, Jo-Ann took me aside and said, "Are you *crazy*? It'll tire her out."

I said, "If we *don't* do this, it will kill her."

We held the second Bash on October 3, sold six hundred tickets and raised $100,000. We started preparing for the third Bash in July 2009. Lindsay was pretty weak by then, but working on the fundraiser energized her. The tumour had spread to new areas of the brain, and doctors found tumour cells in her cerebrospinal fluid and in her spine. Surgery was no longer an option.

Doctors gave her one to three months to live, but she wouldn't accept it. "I'm okay," she told me, even though she was so weak she needed a walker to get around. "I'm passing the test." But it broke her heart later to say, "I may not be able to be there for the next Bash."

I told her that was fine: "If you just want to go for fifteen minutes, that would be fine, too," I added. Well, seven hundred people came that September night and we raised over $120,000. Lindsay was very thin, but being among her friends and knowing she was helping to raise money for research that would help others — it made her strong. She ended up greeting people until midnight, well beyond what we ever thought she could handle.

• • •

October 2009 — Jo-Ann's Story

Lindsay's older brother and his girlfriend announced their

engagement. Knowing how important the wedding was to Lindsay, the couple decided to marry in three weeks, so she could attend the celebration as a bridesmaid. When Lindsay heard her brother's plans, her face lit up. When I asked her, privately, if she thought she could go through the ceremony, she said, "I'll just have to suck it up again."

The wedding day was one of the happiest days of her life. Many of the guests didn't know how sick Lindsay was; she hid it very well.

Next up on the calendar was my birthday — November 16. I didn't feel like celebrating anything, but Lindsay insisted that she and John go get a gift for me. By this time she was so weak that her legs wouldn't support her weight. He was always lifting her: lifting her into a wheelchair so she could manoeuvre around the house, and then lifting her into the car to drive her to the store. She picked out a ceramic tile with a peony on it, and told John, "That's the one I want to get for Mom." She especially liked the tile's inscription, which read, "Twilight worries will be appeased by the ardour of a single bloom." When she gave it to me, she said, "You're a keeper."

It became too difficult for her to navigate the stairs, so we converted the dining room into a bedroom for her. It was a cozy space, with her favourite furnishings surrounding a hospital bed and a space heater to keep her warm. There were all the comforts she'd ever need.

We knew Lindsay's time was drawing close, and we tried to be strong for her. But it was tough. It was so tough. We contacted her younger brother at college and told him that she wasn't doing well and he should consider coming home soon. She was in such rough shape; her pale skin was at times translucent. She was so weak, even keeping her eyelids open seemed like such a chore. We were basically pleading with her to keep going, to stay alive and be strong, because her brother was coming.

When he came, he didn't even take off his knapsack; he just rushed into her room. "Oh, Lindsay," I called, "Michael's here."

"Hi," she said, her voice as soft as a baby's breath.

"Is there anything you want to say to him?" I asked her.

She smiled. "Kick some ass."

The day she passed, November 26, about two dozen of Lindsay's closest friends and family members came by to pay their respects. Lindsay had slipped into unconsciousness the day before, so we knew her passing was imminent. I moved around the house as if I were a ghost: I knew what was happening, but I didn't want to believe it. At times, I wondered if this were a dream, or I had wandered into someone else's life by accident.

Our priest had also stopped by to be with us. Lindsay wasn't conscious, but I knew she could still hear us. We held hands and formed a circle around her to say our goodbyes. The minute all of our hands connected, Lindsay's breathing pattern changed. Her breaths became slower, calmer. We kept talking to her the whole time, everyone saying things like, "You're a great sister," "Lindsay, you're a great friend," and I choked to say "You're the best daughter. Your life means so much to me."

Suddenly, her eyes fluttered.

"Okay, darling, you can let go now," I said, swallowing my tears. I wanted to be as brave as she was these last few months. Others in the circle joined me, until it became like a quiet chant. "You can let go now. You are at peace."

Her eyes opened. My heart soared as I watched her colour change. She became more radiant. She looked up, staring at something, a look of awe on her face. And she seemed … comfortable. Very comfortable. In that moment of peace, I felt touched by God.

Lindsay took three little feather breaths, and then she was gone.

Thursday, November 26 — four days past her twenty-sixth birthday — at 2:03 p.m.

Later, people told me that at around 2:00 p.m. that day, out of nowhere, a rainbow had appeared. A person delivering flowers to the house even commented on how surprised he was to see a rainbow, considering it hadn't rained that afternoon.

• • •

February 2010 — Lindsay's Story

Today, photographs of Lindsay are found throughout the Bolgers' home. She smiles from elegantly framed pictures on the shelves in the den, where we sit tonight, and remember and celebrate Lindsay's life. Our chairs and sofas surround a table, which is graced with a centrepiece of photos of Lindsay.

Jo-Ann points out the ceramic peony tile Lindsay bought for her birthday. "Every time I look at that flower, I think of her," she says. "I almost feel her saying to me, 'Don't worry, mom, I'm in a good place.'"

Lindsay's wake was standing room only. Almost one thousand mourners jammed the funeral home, and my sister, her husband, and I stood in the receiving line for more than an hour before we could give the Bolgers our condolences. So many people wanted to say goodbye to her and wish the family well — all of the friends she had made at school, the acquaintances who befriended her through the Bashes, and the uncountable number of individuals who knew her story and were touched by her courage and optimism.

And Lindsay's compassion continues to touch the world. The three Bashes raised more than $285,000 for brain tumour research. Many thousands more were collected by about 120

Xavier alumni who held a B-Strong Walk in Ottawa in honour of Lindsay on May, 2009.

I met with the Bolgers several times during Lindsay's illness, and always offered to see Lindsay in person, but Jo-Ann said her daughter was afraid of me. I respected that and kept my distance, even though I had wanted to attend a B-Strong Bash to show my support. This year, I will go.

Jo-Ann showed me the notes she made during our talks. I read that in 2006, among other things, I mentioned "a big sigh of relief because of huge change," yet also said, "don't get too excited too fast. Be patient." In January 2008, I sensed blood clots and a fuzzy feeling in her head, yet felt she would be involved in a marriage (after the fact, I realize I was intuiting her brother's marriage).

I remember how awful I felt preparing myself for the meetings. I genuinely cared for Lindsay and the Bolgers, but I always felt such sadness when tuning into their situation. I knew it would not end well. What could I possibly say to give them hope? I knew I could not paint false, rosy pictures. But was I a coward for not giving them the straight truth? I felt helpless, and prayed for help before every meeting with them. And ordered my guides not to show me the Death Angel.

• • •

"Was I able to give you any help at all?" I ask Jo-Ann tonight, trying not to sound like I am pleading.

She is quiet for a moment. John, too, is contemplative.

"The way you presented the information was positive," Jo-Ann says. "You gave us hope. You gave us energy to push to go on. If you had just given us negative news, I would've just wanted to curl up and not keep going."

I thank Jo-Ann for her kind words.

"I lie in bed sometimes at night and hug her pillow, and ask her to send me a sign that she's okay," she says. "But I don't know what I'm looking for."

"Do you ever feel goosebumps?" I ask.

Jo-Ann hugs herself. "Yes. I'm feeling them right now. Up and down my arms."

"That's Lindsay," I say. "She's giving you a hug from spirit."

Jo-Ann closes her eyes and smiles. Perhaps she is seeing her daughter again. The Lindsay that will always live in her memory: the bright, athletic young woman whose future seems like a road that has no end. But, in a sense, that is already true, for Lindsay's story will never end, not as long as people act like compassionate messengers and inspire the world with good work.

I will give Jo-Ann one last message: *love never dies.* Perhaps she knows this already. But it is always good to hear those words one more time.

● ● ●

Would you like to continue Lindsay's story? B-Strong continues to raise money for brain tumour research through its B-Strong caps, Lindsay Bears, and upcoming Bashes; for more information, please visit *www.bstrong.ca.*

Acknowledgements

This book is about spirit. Without the help of my spirit friends (my guides and angels), my friends in spirit (whom I have known here but have transitioned), and a highly respected publisher who passed into spirit in 1971, this book could have never been written. I thank them all. Without their help, guidance, and support, and the love and energy they weave into our lives, I would not have the ability to serve the way that I do.

I am also grateful to those on this side of the veil for their love and encouragement. Many thanks to Margaret at Dundurn Press for taking a chance on me — I hope she hasn't regretted it! And to Dundurn editors Michael and Shannon for their patience and understanding in educating me on this process of publishing, and for Beth's enthusiasm and belief in this work.

Acknowledgements

Jill Segal, my friend and inspired artist, created something truly beautiful for the book cover. Thank you, Jill, for using your intuitive heart to create this gorgeous work. To see more of Jill's work, visit *www.jillsegal.com*.

If it weren't for my webmaster, Bill Dunk-Green, I might never have been noticed by the many people who have read my blog and kept coming back for more. And you know who you are! Thank you, Bill, for a wonderfully clear website.

I would not be who I am today without the wise teachings of my children, Diana and Jeffrey — my incarnate wise ones.

I also wish to thank the thousands of loving, courageous, and insightful people whom I have met along my path. My clients and students have often been my greatest teachers. You have met only a handful in this book. I am especially indebted to the families and friends of Bobby Slash and Lindsay Bolger for allowing me to share their stories; in all other circumstances, names and some details were changed to protect individuals' privacy.

And last, but certainly not least, my heartfelt thanks and love to my husband Benjamin. Without his wisdom as a writer, confidant, and friend, I would never have begun this project. I can put words to paper, but I am no writer — give me a spirit person any day of the week, but please don't make me write about them!

While brushing my teeth the other day, my guides came in so clearly, saying, *You needed to have Ben in your life to make this happen.* So, thank you, "guys," for giving me such clarity. And thank you, God, for sending me such wonderful people to help me make this book possible.

And thank you for reading this book. I hope you enjoyed it! I'd love to hear your comments. Write me at *www. carolynmolnar.com*.

Of Related Interest

Psychics and Mediums in Canada
Jean Porche & Deborah Vaughan
978-1-550024-975
$22.99

Whether you think psychics are limited to 900-line phone scams, or whether you are a believer, *Psychics and Mediums in Canada* is sure to intrigue you. Well-respected psychics, mediums, and readers from across the country — individuals possessing extra-ordinary gifts of psychic insight — are profiled within. You will also find a history of psychism in our country, frequently asked questions, what to expect from a reading and how to evaluate a psychic, and how to develop your own psychic gift.